T0159928

The Challenge
of
Enlightenment

IRH Press

BOOKS
IRH PRESS
New York

ISBN 13: 978-1-942125-92-1
ISBN 10: 1-942125-92-5
Cover Image: Loguna / Shutterstock.com
asharkyu / Shutterstock.com
Texture background wall / Shutterstock.com

Printed in Canada

First Edition

The Challenge
of
Enlightenment

NOW, HERE,
THE NEW DHARMA WHEEL TURNS

Ryuho Okawa

IRH PRESS

Contents

PART ONE

Preface for Part One

CHAPTER ONE

What Is the Spirit of Buddhism?

CHAPTER FOUR

What Is Egolessness?

CHAPTER FIVE
Emptiness and Causality

CHAPTER SIX
Karma and Reincarnation

CHAPTER ONE

Progress through the Middle Way

CHAPTER TWO

Hinayana and Mahayana

CHAPTER FIVE

Egolessness from the Perspective of the Middle Way

Buddha-Nature and Buddhahood

PART ONE

Preface for Part One

The fundamental sutra book of Happy Science is *The True Words Spoken By Buddha*. The basic doctrine is the *Exploration of Right Mind*, and the practical expansion of this doctrine is known as the *Principles of Happiness*, consisting of four principles—*Love*, *Wisdom*, *Self-reflection*, and *Progress*—that are also known as the modern Fourfold Path. The central ideas of these teachings can be summed up in three main concepts: *love*, *enlightenment*, and the *creation of utopia*.

The love I teach is "love that gives," based on the Buddhist spirit of compassion and selfless giving. "Enlightenment" is the manifestation of Buddha-nature of each individual; the different levels of enlightenment correspond to the multidimensional structure of the Real World. The "creation of utopia" comes from Sangha, an order conceived in Buddha's ideal world where a peaceful society is created by people who learn Buddha's teachings.

The ideas of love and enlightenment can be bridged through the philosophy of *the developmental stages of love*, as described in *The Laws of the Sun*.[1] This philosophy unites the civilizations of the West and East. These ideas will become the spiritual pillars for creating a new civilization, an ideal world on a global scale. In this way, the three concepts of love, enlightenment, and the creation of utopia will come together to achieve the ideals of Buddha.

In this book, *The Challenge of Enlightenment*, I have mainly focused on the issue of enlightenment. This is an attempt to cast light on the various teachings of Shakyamuni Buddha, who attained enlightenment in India more than 2,500 years ago, and re-examine them from the standpoint of Truth that Happy Science has currently reached, with the hope of revealing the true meaning of those teachings.

As you read this book, you will see how it highlights the errors: the misinterpretations in Buddhist studies and the mistakes made in the doctrines of various Buddhist organizations.

This book is by no means about the challenge of attaining enlightenment but rather is an attempt to answer questions about the possibilities that enlightenment represents in today's world. Does enlightenment really have the power to take away people's suffering and anxieties and open up a new world for the future? Can Buddha's enlightenment be brought back to life in these times to cast light on the future? Is Buddha's Law worthy of the title "Eternal Law"? Therefore, this book indeed represents not only the challenge of enlightenment but also the challenge of Ryuho Okawa and the challenge of Happy Science.

> *Ryuho Okawa*
> *Master & CEO of Happy Science Group*
> *June 1993*

CHAPTER ONE

What Is the Spirit of Buddhism?

1

The First Turning of the Wheel of Dharma

The Day of November 23 is the anniversary of the First Turning of the Wheel of Dharma at Happy Science. On that very day in 1986, I raised my first voice in Nishi Nippori, Tokyo. There were 87 people in the small, plain room that was only 70 sq. meters. In those days, we had just over a hundred members, and about 90 of them had gathered from all over Japan to hear my first speech.

Since then, I have been doing many things at a rapid pace, and I now feel that my teachings are spreading year by year, as if the wheel of Dharma is turning.

In Buddhist pictures and wall paintings, we often find a wheel painted under a tree. This was used as a symbol because in later years, people were too awed to directly paint Buddha's figure. The wheel is a symbol of Buddha conveying the Dharma or the Law. It implies that the true nature of Buddha is not that of a human being living in a physical body but the Law itself, and the act of teaching the Law itself is the true nature of Buddha. For this reason, a wheel was often used to depict the preaching of Buddha.

When delivering spiritual messages during the early days of my spiritual activities, I received a similar talk from a certain supporting spirit. I had no idea how to explain and convey the enlightenment I attained. One day, that supporting spirit said to me, "It is just like the turning of a cog. No matter how small the first cog may be, as it begins to turn, it will engage a bigger cog. In the same way, the development of Happy Science may be slow initially, but gradually, it will generate a greater force."

Looking back, I feel the words of the spirit were completely true. At times, I worried about what to do, as I thought my own power was not enough, but such worries were groundless. I am now convinced that once the wheel of Dharma begins to turn, it gradually and naturally gathers momentum.

2

The Middle Way
between Pain and Pleasure

About 2,500 years ago, Shakyamuni Buddha had a similar experience. At the age of 29, he left Kapilavastu, the palace that was his home, and for the next six years, he went through all sorts of ascetic training that were popular at the time in India. Although I have referred to him as Buddha, strictly speaking, we should say this was a period of discipline for Gautama Siddhartha because he had not yet achieved his great enlightenment.

He tried living on a single grain of millet each day. He even buried his body, leaving only his head above ground so that he could breathe, and meditated seated on a craggy cliff.

As a result of this ascetic training, he was reduced to skin and bone. One day, he went to the Nairanjana River to try and bathe, but his body was so light that he began to float away in the water for a few feet. He had become so thin that he was carried away like a piece of driftwood, unable to even stand up in the water, and he wondered if he was right to go on living in that way.

Asceticism and self-mortification had made him so weak and frail that he thought, "I will soon die if I continue this way. Am I doing the right thing?"

It was then, as Gautama was on the verge of losing his life, that Sujata, a village girl, happened to pass by and offered him a bowl of milk porridge. This story has been handed down through the ages and has become a legend; the details have been described in different ways. Some say that Sujata offered him gruel made of cream that had been produced by repeatedly boiling down the finest milk; others say the gruel was made of cereal. Whatever the details may be, Gautama accepted a bowl of milk porridge. Gautama was so frail that he could be taken by the river. However, as he ate the porridge, he felt his body fill up with energy and suddenly was revitalized.

Then he thought, "For years, I have tormented my body in pursuit of enlightenment. But if this kind of self-mortification were the true mission and purpose of life on earth, then being born in this world itself would be a mistake. If spiritual discipline means denying life in the physical body, then human beings shouldn't be born into this world. Is asceticism really the path to enlightenment? All seekers of enlightenment in India devote themselves to ascetic training; they try to walk on fire, stand on one leg, and stay awake for many days. Do all these strange practices really lead to enlightenment? Something is not quite right."

So he said to himself, "I will rebuild my body, and with a healthy body, I will seek the truest enlightenment that a human being can attain." After that, he started to accept alms when they were offered, continued meditation, and gradually attained enlightenment.

Up until that time, there were five fellow seekers training with Gautama. They were first the disciples of the hermit Udraka-Ramaputra. However, after seeing how Gautama equaled the master very quickly, they left their master and practiced asceticism with Gautama.

Of the six, Gautama was the most enthusiastic about asceticism and had won certain praise from the others.

However, after he took the offering of porridge from the village girl, the other five began to doubt what he was doing. They talked among themselves: "What happened to him? He seems to have become lazy these days. He just sits cross-legged beneath the pippala tree, absorbed in meditation. Perhaps he is simply idling away his time. He has become a dropout." And they decided to leave him. After that, Gautama attained enlightenment by himself.

Therefore, the first stage of his enlightenment was the realization that in the process of spiritual discipline, it is essential to keep to the Middle Way between pain and pleasure. The path to the Truth is found neither in the pain of rigorous asceticism nor in the pleasures of a luxurious life, like that in the Kapilavastu palace. It is to be found only after rejecting the two extremes.

Well then, what was the enlightenment that Gautama later attained as he was meditating under a tree?

At that time, it was generally believed that attaining enlightenment was synonymous with acquiring supernatural powers through superhuman training. However, Gautama thought that the true meaning of enlightenment was to attain wisdom while living an ordinary human life. He pursued this wisdom intently.

In the following sections, I would like to explain his enlightenment.

3

The Request of the Brahma for the Turning of the Wheel of Dharma

Gautama attained the enlightenment of Buddha under a bodhi tree. For some time, he was absorbed in the bliss of enlightenment—the joy of becoming aware of the Law—as if in a state of ecstasy. He was so happy that he could not move from under the tree, thinking, "Finally, I have attained enlightenment. Nothing can compare to this joy." It is said that he remained seated there for 21 days (some say it was 35).

Eventually, he said to himself, "Even if I were to teach the Truth I just attained, it would be too difficult for others to understand, so I would rather keep it to myself. My enlightenment was attained without any teacher, and the level of it is so high that ordinary people would not understand. I would be content to keep the enlightenment to myself only and leave this world blissfully."

Looking down on this from heaven, the Indian gods known as Brahma, or what I term supporting spirits or high spirits, appeared to him and one of them said, "O Buddha, you look truly satisfied with the joy of your enlightenment, but please do not keep it to yourself. Can you remember why you attained enlightenment? Was it solely for your own joy? But it shouldn't be so. Although it might be very difficult to teach what you have achieved, you must go ahead and teach the Law to save many people. No matter how much you are misunderstood or ridiculed, you definitely need to teach the Law."

The high spirits repeatedly pleaded with him to teach the Law for the benefit of all people.

But each time, Shakyamuni replied, "I hear what you say, but I don't think ordinary people can understand this Law, nor do I want to give up the bliss of this enlightenment. I do not want to move from under this tree."

The high spirits pleaded with him so earnestly to teach the Law that Shakyamuni finally accepted their entreaties.

However, he had no idea to whom to teach the Law. Also, he was worried as to whether there was anyone who would really be able to understand it. Then, the Brahma suggested to him, "Do you remember the five seekers who were with you for years but left? You will find them in Deer Park (present-day Sarnath) not far from Varanasi. Please go there and give the first sermon to them."

So Shakyamuni traveled to Sarnath. When the five other seekers saw him approaching, they said to one another, "It's him. The dropout is coming!"

In those days, it was believed that once a seeker had given up discipline, there was no chance of his returning to the path; such a person was considered a dropout. So the five men spoke ill of him: "Gautama, the fallen one, is coming!

He looks quite healthy. He must have received a lot of alms and gained weight." They quickly agreed among themselves that they would not talk to him.

However, as Gautama approached, they saw a kind of holiness surrounding him. He was emitting a bright light, and they were blinded by it. "What's this? Why is it so dazzling?" They were deeply moved by his divinity and so surprised by his presence that despite the promise they had made, they began to speak to him: "Well, friend! What has happened to you?"

At that time, it was a custom for seekers to address one another as "a friend." However, Gautama solemnly admonished them, saying, "Do not call me 'friend.' I have attained enlightenment and become a *tathagata*. You must not address a tathagata as a 'friend.'"

The five seekers were astonished. "What happened to him? He has become an utterly different person. He seems quite different. He seems to be tremendously powerful, solemn, and divine." They were impressed simply by his dignity. "What sort of enlightenment did he attain? Everything about him seems completely different."

They instantly recognized his status, yet they still could not understand how a dropout could become so elevated. After some moments of confusion, they asked him to explain his enlightenment.

Shakyamuni then spoke earnestly and patiently of the enlightenment he attained under the bodhi tree. First, Kondanya, one of the five seekers, jumped up and shouted, "I understand!" Observing this, Shakyamuni exclaimed, "Kondanya understands!" In this way, Kondanya was said to become the first *arhat*.

At that time, it was not very difficult to become an arhat because all it required was to understand Shakyamuni's teachings, but in later years, the requirement gradually became more rigorous. After Kondanya, Assaji and the other disciples came to understand the teachings one after another.

In Shakyamuni's time, it was common for seekers to focus on ascetic training, so it was not easy for people to understand that they could attain enlightenment through words or ideas. That was why it took some time for the five to understand the situation.

Despite the fact that more than 2,500 years have passed, a similar situation still exists today. In Japan, for example, there are many religious organizations, and the followers of many of these groups still conduct ascetic practices such as walking in the mountains, climbing steep cliffs, and meditating beneath waterfalls. As far as I can see, religion has not progressed very much. Once in a while, an enlightened person appears and teaches the Law, but most of those who seek religious awakening repeat the same physical disciplines in the belief that practicing some superhuman training will lead them to enlightenment.

In Buddhism, the first sermon Shakyamuni preached to his five companions in Sarnath was named the "First Turning of the Wheel of Dharma."

From then on, Shakyamuni and the other five continued discipline together, confirming their enlightenment, and before long, they decided to convey the teachings to laypeople.

The first layman to hear the teachings was named Yasa. He was a slim, fair-skinned and handsome young man, and after he heard Shakyamuni preach the Law, he renounced the world and became a monk. His parents also became followers but remained in the secular world. Lay followers were called *upasaka* (male disciples) and *upasika* (female disciples). From that time on, the spreading of the Law began to gather momentum.

Shakyamuni attained enlightenment at the age of 35 years and a couple of months. He first headed to Sarnath to convey the teachings and that is when the movement started. In this lifetime, I started conveying the teachings at age 30, so I awakened about six years earlier than Shakyamuni.

4

Discovery of the Four Noble Truths

What did Shakyamuni preach at the First Turning of the Wheel of Dharma? What was the content of enlightenment that the high spirits pleaded with Shakyamuni multiple times to teach but were repeatedly denied because he thought it was too difficult? I would like to talk about that now.

Let me explain what and how he taught his five fellow seekers to lead them to the state of arhat.

First, as I mentioned earlier, he taught them the Middle Way as the correct attitude for a seeker.

"First of all, remember the Middle Way. You must avoid extremes. It is not desirable to practice rigorous disciplines to the extent of reducing yourself to skin and bone or starving to death. At the same time, it is not right for you to seek too much worldly pleasure as ordinary people do.

"While applying a certain degree of discipline to yourself, you must live your present life to the fullest. Be strict with yourself, but at the same time, be careful not to be too hard on yourself. If you cause yourself pain, the same kind of pain will await you in the next life. You must avoid doing that. The purpose of your discipline should be to make progress in your character. It is very important to observe the Middle

Way. You must first realize that the Middle Way is the very heart of your discipline.

"It is just like playing the lute. If you tighten a string too far, it will snap, and if it is too loose, it will not make any sound. Only when the string is tightened to the right degree does it sound beautiful. Your discipline is similar. In order to continue making a beautiful sound for a long time, you need to tighten the strings to just the right extent. This is the starting point of your spiritual discipline. You must always observe the Middle Way when pursuing the Truth."

After explaining the attitude that seekers should observe, Shakyamuni taught the Four Noble Truths. The Noble Truths are called *satya*. Therefore, Shakyamuni was enlightened with the Four Noble Truths and that is what he taught to the five fellow seekers.

What are the Four Noble Truths?

First, the meaning of our existence in this earthly world has to be defined. Shakyamuni said that our life on earth is like living in delusion; it is "suffering."

This may sound strange and you may well ask why life is suffering. But I would like you to once again think deeply about this and contemplate it. Suffering, in this case, means the way ordinary people live in this world, ignorant of their purpose and mission on earth. Once they attain enlightenment, however, their suffering disappears and a world of joy unfolds.

Many of you readers may already have advanced quite far along the path to enlightenment, but in this world, there are still a large number of people who know nothing of the Truth. Some completely deny the existence of the other world and think that death is the end of everything. Some believe that human beings have evolved from amoebas, yet others think that human beings are no better than machines.

Such people live recklessly in their later years because of their fear of death. Some think that because they only have a few decades left to live, they will do whatever they like while they are still alive. They give themselves up to the enjoyment of sensual pleasures and get intoxicated, become addicted to gambling, or destroy their families. Some are even reduced to becoming thieves or murderers. They live a destructive life.

It's all because they do not know the proper way to live, the right view of life, and their true purpose and mission on earth. I am sure you will agree that such a life is absolute suffering and that those living in this way are to be pitied.

What happens to these people afterward? Even while they are living in this world, they experience strong negative reactions to what they do, but they must remember that there exist heaven and hell in the other world. In light of the Truth, it is obvious that in another 10, 20, or 30 years, such people will undoubtedly go to hell and suffer if they do not change their present way of life. Unfortunately, however, there is no way to make them understand this. Even if you try to warn them that their future will be awful unless they change their way of life, they will not listen. Rather, they will respond, "Nonsense! I know of no one who has gone to the other world and returned from there. I've never seen a soul. There is no God or Buddha. Don't believe in such old-fashioned stories. Religion preaches to get money, so don't be taken in by it."

Many people will respond in this way, but they will inevitably fall to hell headfirst. To use an allegory, the ogres of hell are waiting for them, ready to boil them in a big pot; however, not knowing this, these people innocently enjoy their life. Although they think they are living quite happily, in light of the Truth, they are actually in an awful situation; it is as if they are on a train that will surely derail. Simply put, suffering is when you are living unaware that you are wrong.

Also, the suffering Shakyamuni taught about is not the kind of pain we usually feel in our everyday lives but the pain of living in this world without a true sense of satisfaction. If we look at things from a worldly perspective, death is a terrible thing and our craving for material things is endless. We want to do everything we desire before we die, but our desires are not necessarily fulfilled, so we struggle. By observing those situations, it seems that suffering includes feelings of dissatisfaction, unease, and sorrow.

In this three-dimensional world of matter, people are apt to make mistakes, and it is hard for them to gain the right view of life. For this reason, Shakyamuni said: "Before you awaken to the Truth, it is as if you are swimming in a sea of suffering. This is the truth of life."

In those days, in India, three kinds of suffering were considered to exist: unquestionable suffering, suffering born of destruction, and suffering born of change.

The first type, unquestionable suffering, is the actual pain or suffering that we unquestionably feel.

For example, this could be the pain caused by hot or cold weather. If you find yourself in a snowstorm in mid-winter in the wilderness, simply being there is suffering. It is very hard to live in a place where there is heavy snow. To live in a tropical jungle, or to work in a desert under the glaring sun, is also suffering. Illness, too, is suffering; everyone suffers when they become ill.

Just like that, unquestionable suffering—the suffering of suffering means that such existence itself is suffering and such existence itself carries the nature of suffering, things that are in no doubt suffering.

The second type of suffering, the suffering that is born of destruction, is the suffering we experience when something breaks down. People suffer when they fall from a certain state or when they see a set of conditions destroyed.

For instance, a married couple may live happily in harmony, but one day some incident may occur that causes ripples in their minds. Then, they begin to quarrel and eventually divorce. They may be separated from their children. A family in harmony breaks apart once and for all.

Another example of the suffering born of destruction is the bankruptcy of a company. Although a company may have been running quite successfully, it may suddenly go bankrupt because of a recession. The workers may have been working quite diligently, hoping to be promoted to higher positions, but if the company goes bankrupt due to things like a shift in the economy, there is nothing the individual can do. When the company collapses, the employees see their previous set of conditions destroyed.

There are many such instances. Often, something that you took to be the source of your happiness is destroyed for some reason or another in a single day. This suffering is born of destruction. I'm sure you can think of many instances like that.

The third type, the suffering born of change, is the kind of suffering we experience because everything in this world changes and nothing remains the same.

In the spring, for example, we enjoy the beauty of the cherry blossoms and feel so happy. We wish we could see them forever. We wish they would blossom in our garden all year round. But in less than a week, sometimes in just three days, the cherry blossoms are washed or blown away as the rain falls and the wind blows. There is no way to keep them as they are.

Human beings, too, go through change. People want to stay young for as long as they can, yet they grow older year by year. Even money can't keep you young. However painful it may be, it is impossible for us to stop ourselves from aging. Some people never want to grow up, but they still become adults. Their parents die, and they are forced to live on their own. Then, they have to work and earn a living. Women, who are attractive when they are young, often suffer as they grow older, adding more and more wrinkles and developing a bent posture. This is painful. This is suffering born of change. Everything is constantly changing, and this causes us suffering.

In sum, it was the wisdom of the ancient Indian people to divide suffering into three kinds: unquestionable suffering, suffering born of destruction, and suffering born of change.

5

The Four Pains and the Eight Pains

Shakyamuni analyzed suffering more deeply than traditional Indian philosophy did, and he classified it more precisely.

He said, "I have told you that life is suffering and that this world is suffering. Now, let me explain the truth about what suffering is."

First, he explained the Four Pains, which are the pains of birth, aging, illness, and death. These terms are often used in Buddhism, so you have probably heard them before.

The pain of birth is the pain of being forced into a situation over which we have no control. Before we are born into this world, we are independent, adult souls that live freely in the Spirit World. But once we enter our mother's womb, we have to stay motionless in the dark until we are born into this world.

I have had many chances to talk with unborn babies. Although it may sound strange, I have the ability to communicate with them. Usually, they cry, "It's so dark. I'm scared. I'm lonely. I wanna get out of here as soon as possible." Although they long to get out, they have to stay in their mother's womb for nine months.

In recent years, a new type of suffering has been afflicting unborn babies. In modern Japan, it is said that about a million babies are aborted every year. I suspect that almost one in every two unborn babies is aborted. One in every two unborn babies is aborted before they are born. This is a terrible situation. In spite of their wish to be born into this world, the incoming souls are frightened that they may be aborted. Whether or not they can be successfully carried to term depends on the decision of their parents. Things like this happen, and you can see how a new kind of suffering appears now.

Even if unborn babies do not have to worry about being aborted, they have to stay confined in the mother's womb for nine months, feeling very uneasy and crying, "It's so dark. I'm scared. I wanna get out of here." They feel uneasy before they go into the mother's womb, but even after entering, they still feel very insecure and wonder whether they can be born successfully this time. Souls at this stage actually have the intelligence of a two- or three-year-old child, so they think about things like that.

The moment a baby is delivered from its mother's body, it cries. Why do babies cry and not laugh at this moment? Perhaps because of the hard time they have had. As they come out of the darkness of the womb, they burst out crying; they have no other way to express their feelings. They cannot do anything on their own, not even crawl.

Compared with the spiritual freedom they were used to in heaven, being born as a baby is a tremendous restriction.

Because experiencing birth into this world is such an ordeal, it demands real resolution. It is just like jumping off a cliff or jumping into a pond from a great height.

Even after a baby has been delivered safely, it is still not certain whether everything will be all right. Children cannot feel confident in themselves until they are about 20 years old. There is also uncertainty about what will happen to their parents. Although children expect their parents to work to support them until they grow up, some parents suddenly die due to accidents, so they may have to be sent to care homes or be adopted. Children may also get hurt; for example, they may not be able to get married as a result of being scalded by boiling water owing to the negligence of the parent. No one knows what is going to happen.

Babies have no freedom and cannot do anything other than cry. Such is the pain of being born; we all experience it at the start of our life on earth.

Next is the pain of aging, which is also hard to accept. When we are young, we only think of growing up, but one day we find ourselves past our peak. Athletes reach their prime in their twenties. Sumo wrestlers usually retire in their thirties to become stable masters and train younger wrestlers; although this seems very early, they have to retire because they can no longer sustain their former vigor. Most baseball players retire in their late thirties. Some office workers are asked to retire when they are around 50–55 years old. Some are even asked to retire around the age of 45. Although they still have another 30 or 40 years to live, they are asked to retire at that age even if they worked very hard for the company. Then, people become conscious of aging; they feel that the autumn or winter of their life is approaching and that they will one day be gone. It is painful.

Our ability to remember things also declines with age. Day by day, some of our brain cells die. We start losing control of our own bodies, we have a harder time remembering names, and our vision deteriorates. In addition, we lose the ability to clearly articulate our words and thoughts. These are the pains of aging.

As we lose our freedom, some of us begin to develop delusions of persecution. They know that they are not responsible for these discomforts, yet they dare not blame God, so they begin to blame their family or other external causes for their pain. An older man may blame his daughter-in-law or his son. He may attribute his unhappiness to the fact that his grandchildren are not clever enough, his house is not spacious enough, his subordinates at the company are not good enough, his salary is not high enough, his retirement pension was not as much as he had expected, and so on. As a human being, there is no doubt that an older person becomes more pitiful compared with their youthful times.

For a woman, the pain of aging is more severe. A woman may have been very attractive in her twenties and her husband-to-be may be deeply in love with her, proposing passionately to her, but after she turns 40, she can no longer hide her age. Although in her twenties, she may have been a beauty queen, children now address her as "aunty." Children are cruel. This is painful, too. It may be a great shock, but she must face reality.

What is more, her husband, who may once have told her that she was the most beautiful woman in the world, may begin having an affair with another woman. The wife then discovers that the other woman is 10 years younger than her. She feels she cannot compete with the younger woman in terms of physical attractiveness, however hard she may try. Although she thinks she used to be prettier than the younger woman, she cannot fight against the flow of time. It is impossible for her to get rid of her wrinkles no matter how hard she tries; the best she can do is apply makeup. All things are subject to change. This cannot be stopped. Despite wishing to stay young or become young again, this cannot be done. There is such a kind of pain.

No one can escape the pains of birth and aging. There are absolutely no exceptions, including you, the reader. Some of you may be clever, may come from good families, may be wealthy, or may be good-looking, but not one of you can escape these pains.

The third pain that Shakyamuni taught is the pain of illness. It is very rare for all family members to remain healthy all their lives. Every year, in Japan, thousands of people die in traffic accidents. If we include the number of injuries during these accidents, perhaps the number will rise to tens or even hundreds of thousands. Some may experience accidents firsthand, whereas others may have family members or relatives who get involved in accidents. In every family, at least one person becomes ill or gets into an accident. Sometimes, you yourself suffer; at other times, your family members suffer. This kind of misfortune is inevitable.

The pain of illness belongs to the category of "unquestionable suffering" that I explained in the previous section. Even if you question why you have become ill or why you do not have an indestructible body, the human body will eventually break down; it is made that way. If you do not eat, you will die of malnutrition; if you eat too much, you will die of obesity. This is how we are: it is an inescapable reality. Similarly, too much exercise will destroy your body, and lack of exercise will make your body weak. Drinking too much will, of course, cause liver trouble. It is difficult to keep our bodies healthy unless we take good care of them. But even if we do take good care of ourselves, we may still experience illness one day. These days, there are many cases where mental stress, rather than physical problems, causes illness.

So you cannot escape from the pain of illness. Shakyamuni himself fell ill in his later years as his body became weaker.

In his last days, he suffered food poisoning and died. Even someone as great as him was unable to avoid the pain of illness.

Next is the pain of death. Perhaps you think that because you have already awakened to the Truth, you will accept your own death calmly. But just imagine how you would feel if you overheard your doctor telling your family that you would die soon—in six months, three months, or one month. Do you think you would really be all right?

Nowadays, very few people die of old age; most die from an illness. In the past, however, there were many who died naturally. I am sure that if you learn the Truth, live every day cheerfully, and have peace of mind, you will be able to die naturally of old age. It can happen that in the morning, after reciting the fundamental sutra book of Happy Science, *The True Words Spoken By Buddha*, you smile and pass away. You will not suffer at all, nor will your family have to look after you for a long time. If you live every day in accordance with the Truth, there is a strong possibility that you will die quite peacefully after reciting *The True Words Spoken By Buddha* in the morning and bidding your family farewell. You will not have to suffer in a hospital, but rather, you will be able to leave this world quite beautifully if you always keep your mind harmonious and live cheerfully, without troubling others. While reciting the sutra, you will feel someone from your family who has already passed away come from the other world to take you back. Then, you will say to the people around you, "Well, I think my time has come. Thank you all for everything," and die. You will be able to experience this.

On the other hand, ordinary people who have not yet awakened to the Truth are always afraid of death. Some even think it acceptable to kill any number of people if it is for the sake of saving their own lives.

It could be said that believing in religion and knowing of the existence of the other world is a way to become free of the fear of death, which is one of the most serious forms of pain we experience in our lives. Staying ignorant of the Truth is to be feared, truly.

In *The Challenge of Religion*, I talked about a professor of religion at a famous national university in Japan who, in spite of being a pioneer scholar in the field of religion, did not know what would happen to him when he died. He became ill with cancer, but he could not imagine what would happen to him after the moment of death, no matter how hard he thought about it. He knew at least that death meant saying goodbye to this world, but he remained ignorant of what would happen after he died. It is a great pity that even a person who had studied religion for many years had no idea what would happen after death.

This shows how happy it is to have the right view of life.

No one can escape the Four Pains—the pains of birth, aging, illness, and death. It is certain that everyone will die.

This prediction will never be wrong. Not one of the readers of this book will be alive in the 22nd century. Most people will die during the 21st century.

Shakyamuni first spoke of such Truth of life.

Besides the Four Pains, there is another set of four pains, which together with the Four Pains make up the Eight Pains.

The first is "the pain of parting from the people you love."

In your life, you may have a close friend you never want to be parted from. You also have your dear mother, father, brothers and sisters, friends, and if you are married, a wife or husband and children. But the day will surely come when you have to part from such beloved, beloved people. It may happen through illnesses or accidents. Some are forced to part from their loved ones while still alive, never to meet again. Some are separated in times of war. Some break off with friends because of differences in thoughts and beliefs. A wife and a husband may quarrel because of differences in religion and faith and then separate. You might break off with old friends solely because you joined Happy Science. You will inevitably experience, at some point in your life, the pain of parting from the people you love.

In contrast, there is "the pain of meeting people you dislike."

For example, had I continued to work in a trading company instead of becoming a religious leader, there would have been many occasions where I would meet unpleasant people. I could have been deceived in a foreign country. There are times when you meet such unpleasant people. But even in the world of religion, I have had to meet people who did not agree with me. It happens. If I had still worked in a trading company, I would never have met these particular people.

Although we have many choices in life, it is very difficult for us to avoid the pain of parting from those we love and the pain of meeting those we dislike. I'm sure you will also experience these over the course of your life.

Then, there is "the pain of not getting what you want." This pain is the most common form of human suffering.

You may want to find a good job but be unable to do so. You may want to be successful in the world, find a good partner to marry, or receive a higher salary. You may want a better house that receives more sunlight. Even if you manage to get such a house, perhaps a taller building gets built beside it, blocking out the sunlight. You may want to pass the entrance examinations for a prestigious university but may not be able to do so.

There are numerous things we want in this world, but because we cannot get everything we want, we suffer. Everyone experiences this pain; there are no exceptions. You will feel this pain every time you desire something that is hard to get.

Looking back at your past, I'm sure you have wanted all kinds of things. However, you have probably failed more often than you have succeeded in getting what you want. If you were allowed to start your life over just as you wish, there would surely be countless things you would do differently. There are tons of things you couldn't get.

But this does not apply to you alone. Everyone wants many things that they cannot have—these desires vary from person to person.

Some people suffer because they do not have a wife, whereas others are troubled because of their wives. There is the pain of not having a good partner. Some people suffer because they do not have a child, whereas others are troubled because their children are not very bright. There is the pain of not having a clever child.

There is no end to the pain of not getting what you want. Even if you get what you want, it does not always guarantee your satisfaction.

The last of the Eight Pains is "the pain of having worldly delusions that come from the five senses." As you spiritually awaken, you will have an aversion to the blaze of physical desires.

You may wonder why you have to get hungry every day. In spite of your recognition of yourself as a spiritual being, you still get hungry at lunchtime. If you miss a meal, to your shame, you may want to eat like a horse, forgetting all human dignity. Even if you try to control your attachment to food, you just cannot stop it. It may be the same with alcohol—finding it too difficult to stop your craving. Such worldly delusions exist.

There is also the problem of sensual desires. Sometimes, the blaze of desire for the opposite sex cannot be easily quenched regardless of whether you are young or old. You may think how peaceful it would be if only you could do without sensual desires. However, such desires derive naturally from the physical body. No matter how much you wonder why you have to suffer and no matter how difficult you feel it is to observe religious precepts, you cannot stop these desires.

So no one can escape the Eight Pains: the pains of birth, aging, illness, death, the pain of parting from the people you love, the pain of meeting people you dislike, the pain of not getting what you want and the pain of having worldly delusions that come from the five senses. As long as you live in this world, you are subject to these pains.

6

The Cause of Suffering

The first five disciples of Shakyamuni (a person was regarded as a disciple when he or she acknowledged another to be a tathagata) understood that life is suffering and that is one Truth of life. So they asked him, "What are we supposed to do? If it is just suffering, then there is just no way to be saved."

Shakyamuni answered: "Yes, there is a way. I have discovered the way to salvation. Although human life is full of suffering, there is always a cause. A certain situation exists because there is a cause. It is essential to discover the cause of your suffering."

The second of the Four Noble Truths is the truth of the cause of suffering. This means to consider all the causes of your suffering or to focus on one core cause—in other words, to know what lies at the heart of the problem.

Let us take illness as an example. The state of being ill is "suffering." If you catch a cold, you naturally suffer. Then, it is necessary to find the reason for your cold; this step corresponds to "finding the cause of suffering." You might think the reason is that you got onto a crowded train and stood next to a person who was coughing or that you walked out into the snow without wearing an overcoat. This is the start of discovering the cause of suffering. "You have a cold; your soul is suffering." This is suffering. "But actually, you are suffering because of what you did. You walked in the cold with no coat, right?" "Weren't you with a person with a cold for hours? That's why you have a cold." This is finding the cause of suffering.

Similarly, you can discover the cause of the pain of not getting what you want. If you are worried about not being promoted in your job, ask yourself why you are not on a fast track for promotion. You may be suffering because colleagues who entered the company the same year as you are being promoted more quickly. However, it is no use complaining about this. Instead, you need to analyze the situation and try to find its cause.

Then, you might realize that you have been defiant toward your boss. Or perhaps you did not study enough at college and spent too much time playing mahjong instead. If this is the case, then no wonder you are incompetent at work. If you are to start studying after getting a job, you must study with all your might, but perhaps this never occurred to you. It is no use complaining when you are already starting to lag behind your colleagues. It was all up to you, not others. You should have changed your attitude toward work earlier.

Similarly, if you fall ill, the reason may be a lack of exercise. Perhaps you were a rugby player at college and used to be quite fit, but since then you may have ignored the importance of regular exercise. As a result, 10 years later, you may have become flabby and weak and may have fallen ill as a consequence. That is your own responsibility.

As these examples show, when you realize that you are suffering, you should find its cause.

7

Eliminating Suffering through the Eightfold Path

The third of the Four Noble Truths is the truth of the extinction of suffering. It means to visualize a state in which your suffering has been eliminated or to have the determination to eliminate the suffering.

For example, imagine what would happen if you were cured of your illness or if you were healthier, better off, or more successful in your career.

Or if you are on bad terms with your spouse, imagine what would happen if you were to reconcile. Try to find a way to get along together and imagine how happy your family will be. Remember how happy you and your children were when you were on good terms with your partner, and decide that you will restore harmony in your family. This is the step of the extinction of suffering, where you wish to remove the suffering.

Now, what should you actually do to eliminate the suffering? In other words, how will you recover from your ill state? The answer is the truth of the Path, the last of the Four Noble Truths, which indicates the right direction. This path is the famous Eightfold Path.

The Eightfold Path was originally taught by Shakyamuni[2], and I am now teaching it again.

The first step is Right View; this involves seeing things in the right way and having right views. Right View does not simply mean seeing things through your own eyes; it means looking at yourself, at other people, and at the world from a spiritual standpoint, from the perspective of the Truth. This is the standpoint of Buddha, the standpoint of true faith.

Next is Right Speech. This is a different order compared with the Eightfold Path we generally hear, but I brought Right Speech earlier for the people of today. Right Speech means reflecting on whether you have been speaking in the right way. There is no end to the misfortune caused by careless speech in this world. You may have seen many examples of this in your office or in your family. The destruction of the family is mainly caused by wrong speech. There are not many cases where a couple divorces because a husband hit his wife with a baseball bat or because the wife threw a frying pan at her husband and injured him. Most families break up because the husband and wife exchange harsh words every day and hurt one another. In the workplace, too, the major cause of problems in human relations is words, the use of abusive language, or speaking ill of others. In modern society, using the right words is very important.

Next is Right Action. Traditionally, Right Action involved observing precepts such as "Do not kill," "Do not commit adultery," and "Do not steal." However, I have interpreted it in a modern way and included right work as a part of Right Action. It means working rightly—doing a job in the workplace properly or doing household tasks in the right way. This is indeed the core of living rightly as a human being.

Then, there is Right Living. This means living a life of faith. Know gratitude in your everyday life. Recite *The True Words Spoken By Buddha* every day and keep your mind peaceful. Live each day in an orderly way and aim to improve yourself while giving yourself precepts to observe.

Right View, Right Speech, Right Action, and Right Living are paths of self-reflection that you can all easily practice.

After that comes Right Thought. It means examining and correcting your state of mind. This is quite difficult to understand unless you study the Truth. Many people disregard the importance of controlling their thoughts; they see this merely as something taught as part of old-fashioned morals. Only after they come into contact with the world of religion, will they realize that what really matters is their thoughts. People who live ordinary lives have difficulty understanding this point because thoughts remain hidden unless we express them. For instance, only when a person speaks ill of others does it become clear that the person's thinking is wrong. Similarly, if you hit someone, others will try to stop you because it's obvious that you are doing something wrong. People who practice religion must be careful of their thoughts even if they are not expressed.

Although there are many ways to practice the path of Right Thought, it is most important to reflect on and remove the Three Poisons of the Mind—greed, anger, and foolishness.

Also, there is Right Effort. It means making an effort to refine and improve yourself every day, to plant the seeds of good, and to encourage them to grow. In other words, it is to aim to sow seeds of good that are in accordance with Buddha's Will and nurture them.

Right Effort also means deciding not to sow the seeds of evil or not to do anything that will result in bad karma in the future. If you have said or done something wrong, try to nip it in the bud. Be careful not to sow the seeds of wrong, and if you have already sown one, try not to let it grow.

Instead, sow seeds of good every day—for example, speaking loving words to others. Use the right and kind words to others, be gentle with them, teach the Truth, and convey the teachings to them. Also, continue to nurture the seed that you sowed. Right Effort means observing these practices with spiritual growth as your goal.

Next, Right Will. Through concentration of will, your life will open up in many ways, so this practice is important.

Concentrating the will also means not being distracted from the path of Truth or from Buddha's teachings. If you are constantly distracted, you will not achieve anything, so it is important to concentrate on spiritual discipline, on the path to enlightenment, and be determined to create utopia on earth. Do not be distracted by worldly concerns, and always discipline yourself. You should also aim to live in harmony with other people.

Right Will also involves self-realization through the use of the power of the will. It means holding an ideal image of yourself, directing your will, and constantly endeavoring to realize your goals. Set the direction of your will. That is Right Will.

The last step of the Eightfold Path is Right Meditation, which means practicing self-reflection and meditation in the right way. Depending on the situation, prayer can be considered Right Meditation. Prayer can also be considered Right Will, but only when practiced correctly may it be acceptable to include it in Right Meditation.

In Right Meditation, you actually practice concentrating your mind as a ritual. It is quite difficult if you are submerged in daily routines, so I advise you to set aside time and after reciting *The True Words Spoken By Buddha*, calmly recollect what you have thought and done during the day. For instance, you may recall that you spoke harshly to your spouse. You may regret your complaints about his or her salary and decide to learn how to be content. It is indeed vital to reflect on everything that needs to be made right.

In addition to examining bad words or thoughts, it is necessary to check whether you have taken any good and positive actions. Check whether you were able to live this day in a way worthy of Buddha's praise, and check whether your guardian spirit would be pleased with every detail of your day, as if they were all visible through transparent glass. In this way, there are many different levels at which to practice Right Meditation according to your level of spiritual growth.

8

The Endless Path to Perfection

So the Four Noble Truths are suffering, its cause, its extinction, and the Path. The last Truth, the Path, refers to the Eightfold Path.

The Four Noble Truths and the Eightfold Path are what Shakyamuni taught on the occasion of the First Turning of the Wheel of Dharma. This was the first step of his enlightenment, but it does not mean that this first teaching was less important than what came later. It is a very significant teaching for all of you, even today.

Let me summarize what Shakyamuni taught at the time of the First Turning of the Wheel of Dharma after attaining his great enlightenment under the bodhi tree:

On the path of spiritual discipline to enlightenment
Observe the Middle Way, denying extremes.
It is important for a seeker to maintain this attitude.
Then, learn the Four Noble Truths:
Suffering, its cause, its extinction, and the Path.
First, you must realize that life is suffering,
That living in delusion on the basis of a wrong view of life
Makes you suffer.
Next, find the cause of your suffering.

Then, be determined to eliminate it
And attain happiness.
To attain this goal,
You have been given the Eightfold Path.
These are the eight signposts pointing the way.
Practice this path every day,
Then you will be able to correct yourself.
The Eightfold Path leads to the Middle Way
And allows you to develop yourself from the Middle Way.
This is the Eightfold Path.

In this way, Shakyamuni first taught the eternal path toward perfection. It is a path that knows no end. This is the meaning of the Four Noble Truths and the Eightfold Path.

This chapter is an important teaching regarding the First Turning of the Wheel of Dharma, so I ask you to please keep it in mind.

CHAPTER TWO

Freeing Yourself from Ignorance

1

The Cause of Sufferings in Life

The word *ignorance* is often used in Buddhism to mean spiritual darkness. It is a state in which there is no light; it is as if you are groping your way on a trackless path or walking in the mountains in the middle of the night. You do not know when you might trip on or bump into something or when something might come flying at you. Everything that you touch ignites fear in you. In a sense, ignorance can also mean a lack of wisdom.

In fact, it is ignorance that causes most of your suffering or worries in life. It is because you are living without the light of wisdom that you suffer or worry about many things, and as you get caught up in them, you often sink into the depths of despair.

So it is necessary to examine what kinds of things derive from a state of ignorance. This is a theme that encompasses all the teachings of Buddhism, so I will not go into a detailed analysis of it, but the classical thinking of Buddhism would say the Three Poisons of the Mind. There are three types of poisons that toxify your mind.

The three poisons are greed, anger, and foolishness. The first is greed or excessive desire. The second is anger, which might also include hatred. The third is foolishness or folly. Buddhism says that the Three Poisons of the Mind delude people and lead them astray. This refers to not only renunciant disciples but also lay disciples. These three poisons are the causes of delusion.

2

The First Poison: Greed

One way of understanding what greed is like is to imagine a stray dog searching through a trash can for food, desperately growling and whining. It seems so desperate and greedy, but this is exactly how avaricious people appear, though usually they themselves do not realize it. Looking at them, others may think, "Why are they so greedy? Why do they covet so much? Why do they look so desperate?"

What makes them so desperate? First, there is the desire for food. Suppose a group of people was eating at a table and exercising good manners. Then comes a very hungry person who begins to make a pig of himself. Naturally, the others would all feel uncomfortable and would not want to continue eating.

There is also lust or sexual desire. Some people have very strong sensual desires; whenever they see someone of the opposite sex, they lose control of themselves, as if they are no longer human. They are the kind of people who cannot keep their desires under control.

There is no end to these desires, such as the desire for status and the desire for possession; greed is the feeling of desperately wanting something.

In short, greed is "love that takes." The opposite of greed—using the terminology of Happy Science—is "love that gives." In other words, it is an attitude of offering or selfless giving. The teaching of offering in Buddhism is a teaching that recommends people to abandon greed.

The nature of greed can easily be understood if you observe other people, but it is usually difficult for us to see greed in ourselves. It is quite hard to see whether your own desires or wishes are more than what you deserve, but it is very obvious to see that in another person. Therefore, you need to make an effort to see yourself objectively by observing other people closely.

3

The Second Poison: Anger

Anger, the second poison, means the tendency to fly off into a rage. It is the anger that you cannot control. Some people are short-tempered and quickly fly into a rage; they lose their temper and do not know what they are saying. Instead of thinking calmly to themselves, "This is something I must express my anger about," they become furious the moment they see or hear something that they deem offensive. This is anger.

Anger has been considered one of the poisons of the mind through the ages. When this feeling arises, the calm surface of the mind becomes disturbed. Consequently, you feel uncomfortable and irritated, and you cannot sleep at night. As a result, you cannot enjoy the company of others and fall into the habit of getting angry easily.

There are people who appear to be clever, look good, and are highly competent at work but are not promoted as quickly as they expect. These people typically have a quick temper. Because this type of person may lose his temper or demonstrate a sudden change of character at a crucial moment in business, he loses the chance to succeed just before the finish line.

So even if someone suggests that he be promoted to a managerial position, the executives might say, "We cannot trust him because he is quick-tempered," "What if he starts quarreling with our clients?" "He sometimes lashes out at his subordinates," or "Sometimes he goes against his boss." Because of these sorts of remarks, the promotion is put off. Therefore, if a person doesn't get promoted despite being highly capable, it is most likely because they are short-tempered.

Anger is an animal instinct. When animals feel threatened, they soon growl, show their claws, or bristle their fur. A porcupine, for instance, raises its quills when it encounters an enemy. A human's anger may be similar; it may be instinctive self-defense, an instinct to protect one's territory from invaders. But if you are able to control your anger, your mind will always be calm and serene. This is the most appropriate state to take on spiritual discipline.

There is, however, an exception to this anger. Up until here, I warned you about personal anger. But there is another kind of anger that can be justified—it is the indignation about social injustice. This is not something that should be dismissed entirely. Without this indignation, society cannot improve.

For example, suppose people are oppressed by years of tyranny or feudalism. Farmers can no longer stand it and society cannot be run properly. Then, people like the samurai of the Meiji Restoration may stand up to start a revolution. In such cases, anger is not always wrong. Under such circumstances, indignation is necessary if it is based on the intention to make the world a better place to live. This also has to do with justice and is something we must never lose.

While it is important to keep personal, instinctive anger under control, you need some level of public anger or rational indignation; without this, society would never evolve.

Many of the religious reformations we have seen throughout history were led by those who stood up thinking that the religion at that time could no longer save the people. This occurred as a result of not personal anger but the energy of rational indignation. So please don't misunderstand this point.

Another exception is admonishing others to educate them. This type of admonishment is different from personal anger or hate. When you see someone doing something wrong, it is not right to let him do it. If a child is doing something mischievous, the father or mother must scold the child so that he will be able to correct his wrongs; otherwise the child will grow up not knowing how to control himself. So scolding those who are still immature to give severe instructions is different from personal anger.

These are the two exceptions to anger as a poison of the mind.

4

The Third Poison: Foolishness

The third poison of the mind is foolishness or folly. Part of the Japanese *kanji* character for foolishness symbolizes "illness" and means ignorance. I believe you all can relate to that in some way.

It could be said that everyone is foolish in some sense, unless you are truly enlightened or truly a buddha. Human beings are imperfect and often make mistakes. However, although you are far from perfect, it is important that you do not become so foolish as to let go of your reason.

The kind of foolishness I am referring to may be compared to the folly of a fish coming up to snap at a fly lure. The fish takes the bait and gets caught. A human being would instantly know that it's bait, but fish are unable to recognize that, thinking that it's food, and get caught. Then, they suffer. They lack wisdom.

The same thing can be said of rat traps. We do not see as many rats nowadays, but there used to be quite a lot of them in the old times. If you set a piece of bait inside a rat trap and leave the entrance open, then voilà, a rat would go in. The rat takes the bait, only to be shut in and then killed the next day. Rats are very cautious and will approach a trap very carefully, but if they feel it is safe to go in because there is no one around, they will go in out of their desire for the food. To human eyes, entering a trap is dangerous, but rats assume that if there is no one around, they would be safe, and because they want the food, they go in. They believe that since there is a way in, there must be a way out. And they are caught because they do not know how the trap works. That is how foolish they are.

Another similar example is cockroaches. They have a habit of going into a narrow space, so if you set such a path for them as a trap, they go in without thinking and get caught. This is another example of foolishness.

So it is easy to understand what foolishness is using other living things as examples, but it is quite difficult to see our own follies. As a consequence, we sometimes fall into traps.

We often hear stories of people who had moved to the city from the countryside and were taken in by swindlers who claimed to have found an easy way of earning money. Also, religious people are said to be naïve and credulous. Because of their sympathy, they tend to be easily taken in.

You must always be aware of this kind of foolishness.

5

The Fourth Poison: Pride

I have just described the Three Poisons of the Mind, which have been famous since long ago, but if you are advancing on the path to enlightenment, there are two other poisons you need to be very careful of. They are pride and doubt.

Pride here means conceit or arrogance, and it usually arises from ignorance. There are several kinds of pride, but here I would like to refer to the two main types of pride that seekers of enlightenment need to be most careful about. The first is the desire to boast about something you have done.

When you succeed in something, you want to show others it was you who did it or your ability that made it possible, although in reality you received help from many others.

People easily overlook how much they owe others. It may be true that you have made tremendous efforts to achieve success and that you have sufficient ability to deserve it, so it may be natural for you to want to boast, but this is wrong in light of the Truth.

Suppose a student studied hard to get into a prestigious high school or university. He is so happy that he tells everyone around him he has made it and he is great. It is true that he did well in school and in the exams, so he deserves the praise of his friends. However, he was able to get into the prestigious high school or university thanks to his parents, his teachers, and all kinds of beneficial conditions such as financial aid and geographical advantage that helped him. If he thinks it was his ability alone that allowed him to succeed, then that will give birth to excessive pride.

Another example would be politicians, who tend to be proud just because they have won an election and can participate in governing the country. Those who are overly proud to be in politics may well lose in the next election due to careless remarks that sound as if they are disregarding their constituency. If politicians are too confident of their own abilities, they will fail.

More than 10 years ago, during the F cabinet, the prime minister himself boasted that people everywhere across the nation supported him. Then, he ended up coming second in the preliminary election for party leader and had to step down from running in the actual election. Although he was predominant in a survey, he ended up second in the membership ballot of the Liberal Democratic Party. This is also the result of his egotism or his excessive pride in thinking that because he is extraordinary and capable, he is guaranteed to win.

The same could be said of people who have succeeded after making strenuous efforts and overcoming hardships.

They tend to boast about how hard-won their success has been, and it often seems that their pride has grown excessively.

Like the example of the students I gave earlier, excessive pride can also be seen in the minds of the parents. When everything is going well for the child, they feel overly proud and may begin to think, "Our child is successful because we provided a good education," or "It's because we are such excellent parents." This is also excessive pride, so they must be careful.

Pride comes from success or achievement, which in itself is a justifiable reason. But pride should be controlled precisely because it prevents you from making further progress. The opposite of pride is modesty, and without modesty, you cannot make further efforts. Excessive pride obstructs you from practicing Right Effort of the Eightfold Path.

There is another similar type of pride called conceit. In particular, when a person undergoing self-discipline attains quite a high level of enlightenment, he tends to become conceited. Since ancient times, this has been a common tendency among spiritual practitioners and is also difficult to avoid. Naturally, when people begin to experience a highly advanced state of mind, they begin to feel confident. If they think they are already enlightened, they tend to be blind to their own mistakes and immaturity. In other words, they become incapable of reflecting on themselves. They criticize and denounce others, and before they know it, they become lost in a jungle and can no longer understand where they are on the path to enlightenment.

Shakyamuni Buddha had a disciple and cousin named Devadatta, who rebelled against Buddha. He and his younger brother Ananda were very bright and had considerable influence on Buddha's order. However, Devadatta felt he should be distinguished from the other disciples partly because he was a cousin of Buddha. What is more, because Ananda constantly attended to Buddha, taking care of him, serving as his secretary, and making himself greatly useful to him, Devadatta grew jealous of his brother. His mind was filled with jealousy as well as conceit.

Because he was quite clever, Devadatta was able to understand the teachings and also instruct others. Eventually, he began saying that he was as powerful as Buddha. Later, as Buddha's order grew and the number of believers increased, many kings in the region devoted themselves to Buddha, offering political and economic support. But Ajatasatru, the notorious King of Magadha, admired Devadatta and gave him all kinds of treasures. Devadatta then began to feel elated and mistakenly thought he was powerful enough to form his own sect, which he did. He eventually became corrupt and ended up in hell, of course.

Although he had been one of Buddha's most excellent disciples, he became full of conceit and jealousy and then fell from grace. He couldn't stop being conceited, but if he had been humble, even at the very last minute, he wouldn't have ended up that way.

In Happy Science, too, as members study the teachings, some may begin to feel as if they know all about the world. For example, those who are in the position of teaching or leading others tend to feel they have become very wise and powerful. It may be true that they know more about religious teachings than ordinary people do, but there are many people who know more about the world and have broader life experiences than they do. Despite this, when they are given the title of lecturer or facilitator status, they tend to feel they are better than others because they think they have a "universal" passport. When this happens, they make mistakes; they may embark on undertakings beyond their abilities and eventually fail. So they must be very careful about that.

6

The Fifth Poison: Doubt

In addition to the four poisons of greed, anger, foolishness, and pride, there is doubt, the fifth poison of the mind. In modern society, having questions or doubts is often considered good because a scientific or journalistic approach begins by asking questions, which leads to answers. Modern philosophy has also attached much importance to the exploration or pursuit of questions and the analytical observation of things. So questioning everything is generally considered reasonable.

However, here we have a major problem in relation to the world of faith. Religion is, after all, all about believing. To have faith is to believe in what is invisible. The mind and soul are invisible; God and Buddha are invisible; the light of the great universe is also invisible. We cannot see love with our eyes, nor can we see mercy. All of these things belong to the world of the unseen, and believing in them gives humans nobility. In contrast to animals, human beings can have faith, which gives rise to human dignity.

Therefore, although it is good to ask questions as an approach to learning or research, if this leads to the habit of doubting everything, then there is a chance of you losing what is most precious, the most valuable fruit that life has to offer.

In autumn, when the grapes are ripe, we enjoy their sweetness. But if, before you eat them, you become overly concerned and start questioning yourself, "What kind of grapes are these? Were they fed enough water? Were they grown using chemicals?" or you peel the grape and inspect the inside, you will lose the chance to enjoy them. Being too full of doubt is rather like this.

Although it is important to have the mindset of exploring the questions you may have, it should not be done in a way that would make you lose the most important thing. If your mind is always filled with doubt or suspicion, you can never be serene or calm inside; it is impossible to live with a peaceful mind. If you always doubt others, you will never be able to find peace of mind. It is true that people may attempt to trap or cheat you, but while keeping in mind that such things do happen, generally speaking, it is important to believe in other people.

The five poisons of the mind are different manifestations of ignorance. I advise you to take fact as fact and gain knowledge, examining yourself deeply so you can free yourself of these poisons.

7

The Five Poisons of the Mind in the Novel *Kokoro*

There is a famous novel by Soseki Natsume (1867–1916) entitled *Kokoro* (meaning "heart" or "mind" in Japanese). This book is very popular in Japan, and I watched a dramatized version of it on TV a while ago. When I read the novel as a student, I found the sentences exquisite, and I was deeply moved by its literature; but this time, as I saw the drama from the standpoint of someone who teaches the Truth, I was struck by an odd feeling.

Let me briefly summarize the story. The narrator, a young man, meets an old man who he calls *sensei* (teacher). He is well-educated, and the young man often goes to see him. One day, sensei begins to talk about his past which torments him.

The whole story of his past is revealed later in the form of a will, and he eventually kills himself.

According to the will, back when sensei was a university student, he lived in one of the rooms of a house owned by a widow and fell in love with her daughter. One day, one of his classmates named K, the son of a Buddhist priest, came to live at the house. Having been disowned by his father for switching his major from medicine to literature, K could not afford to pay his tuition. Sensei, who was K's friend, generously offered to finance his stay. But after a while, K also fell in love with the widow's daughter.

One day, K asked sensei, "Do you love her?" He replied, "No, not so much." So K continued to suffer over his thoughts for the girl.

However, sometime later, sensei could no longer contain his feelings and ended up asking the widow for her forgiveness to marry the girl. The widow easily accepted his confession and gave him permission to marry her, but on hearing the news, K was shocked to the point where he killed himself.

After K died, sensei and the girl married, but they were not blessed with children and were unhappy. Eventually, Emperor Meiji dies and General Nogi kills himself over the death of his lord. On hearing this news, sensei leaves the letter for his young friend (narrator) and also kills himself.

It is a simple story.

When I read it back then, I understood that it was a story about love and the inner struggle experienced in youth. But this time, as I watched it on TV, I felt differently and made many discoveries.

Regarding K, the son of a Buddhist priest, I used to think that, "It's not nice to say bad things about people who died" and "K had a pure heart." However, I see things differently now.

Earlier, I talked about the five poisons of the mind. Firstly, in the story, I found greed in K's mind. After being disowned by his father, he had no economic foundation, and his friend offered to financially aid him so that he could live in the house. Although he had no money, had been disowned by his father, and had not yet finished his degree, K contemplates marriage. This is a kind of greed, a desire beyond his means. Without economic independence or a job, it is much too early for a man to get married and start a family. K was the son of a Buddhist priest, so he gave off a mood that made people think he was undergoing stoic and ascetic training, but in reality, he had such greed.

K was also guilty of anger. He took revenge on his friend for betraying him by committing suicide. Although that action may have satisfied him, his friend and the girl had to suffer for a long time on account of his death. In a sense, K haunted them like a possessing spirit, and of course his anger cannot be justified. The anger came from K's own ignorance, so it cannot be justified.

There was also foolishness in his mind; he did not seem very wise. As a student, he found a house to live in and happened to meet a pretty girl there, fell in love with her, and wanted to marry her, but this is as simple as a fish that tries to snap at a worm. He was naïve, that's all. If he had graduated, he would have found many girls who were more suited to be his partner. If he had studied the teachings of Happy Science, he would have learned the ideas of positive thinking and invincible thinking, among many others. However, he came from a family that had inherited a Buddhist temple and thought of himself as more enlightened than others, though actually he was not. In fact, he had no wisdom in the truest sense of the word.

Moreover, K suffered from pride. His friend, sensei, had the tendency to torment himself and was severely critical of himself, whereas K believed that because he had been brought up in a Buddhist temple, he was spiritually developed and wouldn't fall prey to desires. Even so, he easily gave in to his desires, and this led to his suicide. I think this is an example of pride.

Finally, there was doubt. K had doubts about his friend, doubts about the widow and her daughter, doubts about his parents, and doubts about the world. His mind was filled with all sorts of doubt and suspicion, so he was under the delusion that everyone was plotting to persecute him.

Suppose K had proposed to the girl first. Would his proposal have been accepted? Probably not, considering the fact that he had been disowned by his parents, had no ability to make a living, and was living off of his friend. Despite that, he suspected his friend of betrayal and was stressing over what everyone thought of him. Here, we can see an example of doubt in him.

K had all of the five poisons in his mind: greed, anger, foolishness, pride, and doubt. He eventually killed himself, and from a spiritual point of view, someone like him would naturally fall to hell, the cause being in his own mind. Unless he gets rid of those negative thoughts, he will not be able to return to heaven. Neither the friend nor the girl, who later became the friend's wife, is to blame; it is his own fault. It is his own problem.

There are many people like this in hell. They are the kind of people who blamed others or failed to solve their own problems before they died. But such things are indeed something they must overcome, and the reason they cannot do that is none other than their own weakness or ignorance itself. It means to be "without light." You must be aware of that.

On the other hand, sensei married the girl but led a depressing life without children and finally killed himself. Now, what can we find in his mind? He does not seem to be very greedy; his desire seems quite normal. How about anger? Although he is slightly angry with himself, he never flies into a rage. How about foolishness? He does not seem very foolish; he is a well-educated man. What about pride? He does not seem conceited. There is, however, doubt in his mind: doubts about himself, doubts about other people, and doubts about his uncle—that his uncle deceived him about his property at the time of his father's death. He could not trust other people, and this doubt led to his self-distrust, which eventually led to his suicide.

So from the perspective of the Truth, one of the two main characters in *Kokoro* suffers all of the five poisons, whereas the other suffers one. You will be able to tell these kinds of things.

Most of life's problems are rooted in ignorance. It is important to learn the teachings of the Truth to free yourself from ignorance. It is not enough to learn the Truth only through reading: you also need to understand it deeply through experience. This means that you must develop the ability to solve the various problems you encounter in the course of your life. Otherwise, knowledge of the Truth will not turn into true wisdom.

However, there are many people who can score full marks simply on paper. You can acquire knowledge if you have a good enough memory and sufficient time, but the key is how much knowledge you are able to apply to everyday life in terms of your actual experience. Unless you can master this, you cannot truly free yourself from ignorance.

I hope this chapter will help you solve your own problems by yourself.

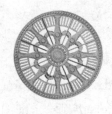

CHAPTER THREE

The Four Noble Truths

1

The Philosophy of Suffering

In this chapter, I will discuss the basic teachings of Buddhism and explain some traditional Buddhist terms, which will help you understand how you can advance on the path to enlightenment.

"The Four Noble Truths," the title of this chapter, is one of the most fundamental teachings of Buddhism. The Four Noble Truths are suffering, the cause of suffering, the extinction of suffering, and, finally, the path to the extinction of suffering. These are four kinds of wisdom.

Buddha taught that through understanding and practicing these four truths, people would be able to enter the path to true happiness. I did not touch on this theme in the first few years of Happy Science because the concept of suffering is quite difficult to interpret.

This teaching appears to be quite different from the Principles of Happiness currently taught at Happy Science—the principles of love, wisdom, self-reflection, and progress.

The Fourfold Path of love, wisdom, self-reflection, and progress has quite a positive and constructive way of thinking in it. First is the teaching of "love that gives," followed by the modern teaching of deep wisdom or insight that comes from studying the Truth. The teaching of self-reflection may not be very different from the traditional teachings of Buddhism. But there is also the teaching of progress, which was not taught so much by Shakyamuni Buddha. In particular, the part about love and progress cannot be straightforwardly understood from the Four Noble Truths. That is why I did not touch on the Four Noble Truths while I taught the modern Fourfold Path. This is the real reason.

Now, let me explain the Four Noble Truths, one at a time.

First is the truth of suffering. Anyone who has studied Buddhism would be well aware of this. Shakyamuni Buddha said that suffering is indeed the truth of life. He said that suffering is the essential nature of this world. But this may sound a little strange to those who are studying our teachings now. You may think, "Is that true? Is Ryuho Okawa teaching us such things?"

They think that way because they have studied the Truth and their awareness has considerably changed. As a basic premise, such kinds of people are already swimming in the vast ocean of the Truth. They are reading numerous books of Truth and attending lectures, seminars, and so on to study the Truth. They enjoy studying the Truth and have already attained the state where happiness wells up more and more by knowing the Truth. To these people, the statement, "Suffering is the Truth. Life is suffering. This world is suffering," will sound quite strange.

However, take a look at the people who have never even thought about the Truth. Look at how they live. You may do missionary work or talk about the Truth to others, but many of them neither want to listen nor understand it at all. If you observe the way such people think and the way they live, you will clearly understand the meaning of "suffering" that Shakyamuni Buddha taught.

It is as if you are watching animals that lack wisdom or fish that are about to be caught by a fly lure. Most people do not know that they came from the Real World and don't even think that they will go back there; they believe that life in this world is everything and become immersed in everyday life and the material world. On seeing this, their life is indeed suffering.

This world is a wonderful place to live in and is a Buddha Land for those who have had scales fall from their eyes and have awakened to the Truth. However, if you observe the people who do not know the Truth, or people who are living a life that goes against the Truth, you can really understand that their lives in this world have quite a heavy suffering. They think and act in a way that would undoubtedly lead them to hell. They brush away the saving hand of Truth, wanting to live in their own way, which makes you wonder, "Why won't they understand?"

2

The Four Pains:
Birth, Aging, Illness, and Death

As we have seen, Shakyamuni Buddha's teaching that says "life is suffering" is rather like an eye-opening phrase of Zen Buddhism. When a person who is enjoying a worldly life hears someone say that life is suffering, he may wonder why life is suffering and ask himself, "That's ridiculous. How can that be?" Then, he eventually awakens to the fact that the answer lies in the Four Pains: birth, aging, illness, and death. Please think carefully about this.

First is the "pain of being born." Before being born into this world, we lived as mature and free spirits in heaven. But when we are born into this world, we must first enter our mother's womb and stay curled up for nine months, just waiting patiently in the darkness and not knowing what kind of life awaits us. It is through our mother's pain that we come into this world. Moreover, for about a year after we are born, we can do nothing but cry; we cannot walk or express our feelings in words.

Although we enjoyed freedom as spirits in heaven, birth takes away all of that freedom. In a way, this is nothing but suffering. Spirits are essentially free and without attachments, but such things are dismissed once we are born. We can do nothing with our own free will. We are born in a way that is completely dependent on others, and even after birth, we burden our parents and grandparents. Perhaps a parent may no longer be able to work or get any sleep at night as they try to take care of us as a baby. In such a way, human beings are born to naturally burden other people.

Next is the "pain of aging." You can use the following words to describe this pain to others: "Perhaps you are now young and spend your time enjoying yourself, but human beings will surely age. Look at the old woman with a bent posture. Look at the old man who is now on his deathbed. This is how you will look in several decades. Old age is drawing near, day by day. Don't you realize that?"

As you age, you lose your freedom in the same way you did as a baby. You cannot move your hands or legs as you would wish, you have back pain, you begin to lose your eyesight or your hearing, and you become senile. Although you may have studied hard and worked diligently, you become feeble and lose freedom. If life truly ends with just your body becoming paralyzed due to old age and while awaiting death, then aging is unbearable suffering.

The third is the "pain of illness." Everyone becomes ill in the course of their life, whether it is mild or serious. In some cases, the illness may affect your entire body, which places a great strain on both you and your family. You become unable to live by yourself and suddenly find that you are able to live thanks to the efforts of many other people. But by the time you realize this, you are in the midst of suffering. You cannot escape from that.

Finally, there is the "pain of death." In your thirties, forties, or fifties, you may feel you can keep going as before, but eventually, you will have to face the moment of death. What will happen when you die? Some books, manga, and movies now depict more about life after death, but most people do not know what will actually happen when they die.

When they realize they only have a few years left to live based on the average life expectancy, they cannot suppress their fear of death and repeatedly say, "I don't want to die." Nevertheless, death comes without exception. Death comes to everyone—to kings, doctors, and even religious leaders. It comes to schoolteachers, too. It comes to blue-collar workers as well as white-collar workers. It comes to those with and without the biggest title. It comes to both the wise and the foolish. You might think it would be wonderful if you could attain an undying body through acquiring wisdom, but that is impossible. No one can escape death.

So teaching the Four Pains of birth, aging, illness, and death to those who live frivolously and spend their time in pleasure is an act of removing the veil that covers their eyes or an act of awakening them.

What we can actually find through understanding these four pains is that all things in this world are changing and, therefore, impermanent. We realize that everything we experience in this world is transient and ephemeral.

What kind of thoughts will arise from the realization of the ephemeral nature of this world? You may start to ask questions such as, "Isn't there a way of life that is not subject to change?" It means you will awaken to the spiritual life, become aware of the Will of Buddha, and yearn for an otherworldly way of life. Only after you are faced with the truth of the Four Pains can you reject a view of life that says happiness mainly comes from physical pleasures and begin to affirm the spiritual life. That is the important thing.

The true intention of Shakyamuni Buddha was, therefore, not to tell people that there is no such thing as dreams or hope in this world but to bring a sudden change to their minds full of attachments. This is the very reason he first taught, "Life is suffering. This world is suffering. Suffering is the Truth." In a way, no other thought is as challenging as this.

3

The Eight Pains

Suppose you met someone who was healthy, wealthy, and of high status, and you said to this person, "Life is suffering. Are you aware of this?" They would naturally reply, "What? Why is life suffering?"

Then, you could answer:

"There are the pains of birth, aging, illness, and death. Can you escape these? What about your family? Even if you have a fortune, a good build, good looks, you come from a good family or you have a high academic background, regardless of all this, you cannot escape the Four Pains. No one can escape them." But the person may respond, "Birth is an old event in the past, so we cannot do anything about that. Aging is something I will worry about when I grow old. As for death, I will think about it when the time comes. And I am not ill yet, so I have nothing to do with that."

To someone like this, you could present the next set of four pains: the pain of parting from the people you love, the pain of meeting people you dislike, the pain of not getting what you want, and the pain of having worldly delusions that come from the five senses—in other words, the flame of your physical desires is burning like wildfire and you cannot control it.

If you present these pains, they won't be able to deny you.

At times, you must part from the people you love, such as a lover, a friend, your parents, or your children. This is agonizing.

Furthermore, you experience the pain of meeting people you dislike. Almost everyone experiences this pain. Both you and the other person are thinking, "I don't like this person," but such kind of suffering: meeting someone you dislike, exists.

The pain of not getting what you want is something you experience countless times in our present age. There will be many things you want, but you cannot always get them. This is perhaps the source of most of your suffering.

Finally, there are physical desires. It is difficult to suppress the flames of desire that arise from the physical body. Even if you know that human beings are essentially spiritual beings, you can do nothing about your physical desires. At noon, you get hungry; in the evening, you want to eat dinner and get some sleep; in the morning, you do not want to get up; when you see someone of the opposite sex, you get aroused. Many such thoughts come and go; these make you wonder whether they are really the voice of your soul. You cannot deny the thoughts that derive from your physical body.

No one can escape from the Four Pains and the Eight Pains. They apply to almost everyone. At least one of them will apply to you, and in principle, all of them will.

Now, do you understand that life is suffering? If you do, then change and correct your mind from now on and study the Truth. That was the teaching of suffering.

4

The Eightfold Path:
the Path to the Extinction of Suffering

So far, we have looked at the first truth, "Life is suffering. The world is suffering." Next, let us go on to the second truth, which is about finding the cause of suffering. You must find and understand its cause by objectively analyzing the situation. This is the second step of the Four Noble Truths.

In my books, lectures, and seminars, I often talk from different angles about the reasons people worry or suffer. To become happy, you must first get yourself out of suffering when you realize you are in the midst of it. The first step to getting yourself out of it is to look for the cause or the reason why you are in such suffering.

It is fairly easy for us to spot the faults in other people, but it is much harder to see ourselves objectively, so we must deepen our studies and ask others for advice.

In Chapter Two, we learned the Three Poisons of the Mind—greed, anger, and foolishness—and that all of them derive from ignorance. These poisons of the mind represent worldly delusions.

In Buddhist terms, "worldly delusions" is generally used to mean the negative workings of the mind. There are many kinds of worldly delusions, and most of them arise in relation to the physical body or from wanting to live in a worldly way. If you are caught up in worldly delusions, where do they come from? You should explore them thoroughly to find the root cause of your suffering. Once you find the root cause, you can quickly find the solution.

This is very similar to the process by which a doctor diagnoses a disease. The doctor first examines the patient to see what part of the body is malfunctioning (the heart, stomach, etc.), whether the person has just caught a cold, and so on. In any case, the doctor must see what is wrong with the patient before he can determine treatment.

He then decides whether surgery is required or whether the disease is curable by means of medicine or diet. Whatever the treatment, the doctor must first find the cause of the illness. This is the second of the Four Noble Truths: finding the cause of suffering. And when you pursue the cause, you will find that wisdom of the Principles of Happiness will be helpful.

The third truth of the Four Noble Truths is the "extinction of suffering." Once you have realized that life is suffering and have found the cause of your suffering, you must make up your mind to remove the cause or aspire to get rid of suffering. This is the extinction of suffering. You have to be determined to overcome it. You need to have the willingness to remove the cause of your suffering. You must strive to get rid of your worries. Unless you are determined to do so, you cannot enter the path to happiness.

So you must be determined to eliminate your suffering. Life is like a workbook of problems to be solved. Although a problem may seem difficult to solve, you have to be determined to solve it somehow.

Now, how can you eliminate your suffering? The answer is the Path, the last of the Four Noble Truths; it means the Eightfold Path.

Of the Four Noble Truths, greater emphasis is placed on the last two, the "extinction of suffering" and the "Path to the extinction of suffering." The purpose of the teaching of the Four Noble Truths is to recommend to people that once they become aware of their suffering in life, they should make the resolve to practice the Eightfold Path.

Here, again, I will briefly explain the Eightfold Path. For full details of the path, please read *The Laws of the Sun* (New York: IRH Press, 2018) and *The True Eightfold Path* (New York: IRH Press, 2021).

The first path is Right View; this means seeing things correctly.

Traditionally, Right Thought comes next.

Then, there is Right Speech.

Next is Right Action. The word *karma* originally meant action; your actions create your karma.

Next is Right Living. Here, you check whether you are making full use of your life each day as a child of Buddha.

Then, there is Right Effort. Have you made diligent efforts? Merely living as you are is something even animals can do. It is important to check whether you are making an effort to make further progress every single day.

After that comes Right Will. You check whether you are focusing your will in the right direction, whether you have the will to abandon wrong thoughts and walk Buddha's path, and whether you have a good life plan that will lead you to a better life.

Finally, there is Right Meditation, the right way to practice meditation. There are various practical methods of meditation, including self-reflection and prayer.

This is the traditional explanation of the Eightfold Path, but in the past, I grouped these eight steps in relation to the theory of the developmental stages of love taught in Happy Science.

First, Right View and Right Speech correspond to the stage of fundamental love. Right Action and Right Living correspond to the stage of nurturing love, whereas Right Thought and Right Effort correspond to the stage of forgiving love. I have restructured the eight steps and called the path the True Eightfold Path. You can also call it the New Eightfold Path. This classification of steps may help you practice the Eightfold Path more easily.

For modern people, Right Thought is rather difficult to practice, so it may be easier for you to leave it until later and first reflect on the more practical steps, such as your way of seeing things, your words, your actions, and your way of life; after that you may proceed to check your inner world.

Note that some Buddhists take Right Thought to mean Right Aspiration. This may make Right Thought easier to understand for some people: Right Thought could mean to live with aspirations that well up from the depths of the heart. After all, Right Thought is a way of thinking that creates the right outlook on life.

5

Surpassing the Teachings of Shakyamuni Buddha— To the Great World of Light

So far, I have explained the Four Noble Truths. Let me now explain the difference between the teachings of Shakyamuni Buddha and the teachings of Happy Science on the Four Noble Truths. Please be aware that we are still in the midst of finalizing our teachings.

According to the teachings of Shakyamuni Buddha, the Four Noble Truths and the Eightfold Path are the starting point of spiritual discipline. But his teachings have changed quite considerably over a period of 45 years expounding the Law.

Early on, his teachings mainly focused on the pursuit of the enlightenment of the individual, as seen in the teachings of Hinayana Buddhism. Later, however, as the Sangha grew bigger and its reputation spread, many kings of Indian states such as Bimbisara of Magadha, his successor Ajatasatru who converted to Buddhism, and King Prasenajit of Kosala pledged their devotion to Buddha. This gave Buddha and the Sangha more confidence. As the order became the most influential religious group in India, Buddha began to give teachings that emphasized more positive aspects of the world. The Lotus Sutra includes these types of teachings taught in Buddha's later sermons. The sutra stresses a positive and constructive way of seeing the world.

Whereas his earlier teachings were about the truth of suffering in life and the difficulty of freeing oneself from it, he later made a 180-degree turn and emphasized the positive significance of this world, saying, "All things of this world, not only human beings but also plants and animals, have Buddha-nature within. The Energy of Buddha is inherent in all living beings without exception."

Furthermore, he assured each of his disciples of the attainment of buddhahood in the future, saying, "Although you will only reach the state of arhat in this lifetime, in the next life or in one of your future lives, you will surely become buddha or tathagata." He gave words of hope to his disciples.

He also assured women that they could attain enlightenment in the future too, despite the belief in those days that it was difficult for women to do so. Moreover, he stated that even wrongdoers like Devadatta would be able to attain enlightenment someday.

This is proof of great success. The Sangha attained great success: they gained a considerable amount of trust from society as well as became a huge organization, earning substantial respect. It is then when proactive, positive thinking appears that develops into success theory. What it means is that the Sangha had enough capacity and confidence.

At Happy Science, I have already taught many philosophies of this type. For example, there is positive thinking, the attitude of trying to focus on the bright side in every situation in life, and there is invincible thinking, the attitude of learning lessons from both good and bad things. Advanced thinking is another teaching that urges you to re-examine your way of life from the standpoint of the Real World so as to be able to spiritually raise yourself to the highest possible level. Beyond the teachings of the Eightfold Path are other such positive and affirmative thinking philosophies, which allow you to beat back the suffering in life and achieve greater happiness.

Whereas it took some decades for Shakyamuni Buddha to reach the stage of the philosophy of positivity, Happy Science was more inclined to the philosophy of success from the beginning. We have quickly surpassed the early stage and are at a more positive phase. First was the denial of this earthly world and a worldly way of life, followed by a shift to affirming this world and a life in this world. This is a change in perspective from the standpoint of the weak to that of the strong.

It is also a transition to an attitude for actively generating positivity in this world. The focus of our teachings is on these sorts of powerful thoughts.

It is often said in the mass media that as a religious group, Happy Science does not seem to be very concerned with ordinary problems such as poverty, illness, and conflicts, but our approach signifies that we are already at the next stage of teachings. We started our activities at the level of Shakyamuni Buddha's later years and are now continuing to move to a higher level. This is our standpoint. Please understand well this difference between Shakyamuni's order and Happy Science.

There is no need to repeat the same thing twice. Using the work that was done before as a stepping stone, we are building a higher structure. This is the natural course of events. I have explained the Four Noble Truths in relation to the teachings of Happy Science. I hope you understand this well.

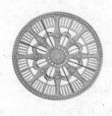

CHAPTER FOUR

What Is Egolessness?

1

A Scholar's Misinterpretation of the Idea of Egolessness

In this chapter, I will discuss the problem of egolessness and ego.

First, let me tell you why I feel the need to offer a detailed explanation of this.

The other day, I was reading a book written by a well-known Japanese Buddhist scholar, Professor U of the University of Tokyo, who was highly influential in academic circles in his lifetime. He took Japan's religious world by storm by establishing an original theory in which he stated that the theory of causality was the central teaching of Buddhism. While I was reading the professor's book, his spirit came to see me. To my surprise, he came not from heaven but from hell. He tried to talk to me, so I spent the night talking to him.

He was a scholar who even compiled his research into a complete set of Buddhist teachings. Therefore, he knew much more about the many academic interpretations of Buddhist theories than I did. He had studied all the original Buddhist sutras as well as all the translations and commentaries on the teachings, and he had established his own unique theory. But since his death, he has been in hell and does not know how to get out of there. It is pitiful to have studied Buddhism and researched Buddhist teachings only to end up in hell. He said to me, "I don't know why I am in a place like this, although I studied Buddhism so diligently."

I thought it was natural that he was unable to understand. Because he accomplished such great work and was well versed in Buddhism, he must have thought he knew everything there was to know about it.

But as I listened to him, I discovered exactly why he was lost: it was his misinterpretation of the idea of egolessness. Although there might have been other points on which he was mistaken, it seemed to me that the cause of his delusion lay in his misunderstanding of this concept.

However, this misunderstanding did not originate from his own thinking. If you study modern Buddhism, you may encounter an interpretation of the teachings that states that because Shakyamuni Buddha preached egolessness, there is essentially no such thing as the self. This interpretation has been widely accepted among Buddhist scholars; even the monks in Buddhist temples seem to think the same. But if this interpretation were right, it would result in the idea that if you attained enlightenment through spiritual discipline while you are alive, then after death, the self would vanish and you would be able to escape the bondage of reincarnation. Because the self disappears, there would be no subject to reincarnate. In that case, you will become clueless about what would happen to yourself in the afterlife. If misunderstood, the idea of egolessness may lead to this conclusion.

When I was talking with the spirit of the famous scholar, he said, "Because there is essentially no such thing as the self, there cannot be any life after death." So I asked him, "But you are talking with me now. Then, who are *you*?" He answered, "Well, I don't know." Because he had also studied Zen Buddhism, he tried to explain his present state of being in a complicated Zen way, saying, "Because there is essentially no self, after death, the self cannot exist. This self is deluded and is not the true self." I said to him, "Regardless of whether the self is deluded, you are yourself. It is *you* who is lost." He continued to develop his argument based on his own peculiar logic, but that will never save him.

There is no denying that there was some mistake in his basic understanding of Buddhism. This is, however, not his problem alone but a problem that greatly affects all Buddhist circles and the whole religious world. I estimate that about half the scholars of Buddhism and religious studies agree with the ideas of this scholar.

2

The Individuality of the Human Soul

It is true that of the Three Dharma Seals that Shakyamuni Buddha expounded, the second seal is the egolessness of all phenomena.

This can also be expressed as "all dharmas are without self." *Dharma* here does not mean teaching or Law indicating the right way of living but rather the whole of creation. It includes all things and all the phenomena that exist in this universe.

So the second seal is the idea that all things are essentially non-substantial and that therefore there is no self or ego in anything made of matter. If you take this idea literally, there is a danger of you thinking, "Because there is no self or ego that is substantial, in the end, everything will disintegrate and disappear into thin air." Although this understanding may be right from the standpoint of the physics of Buddha's Light, which asserts that all things are originally made of light, it cannot be considered right from the perspective that all human beings, animals, and plants are undergoing spiritual training in this world.

This understanding cannot be considered right because each human soul has its own individual character, which actually exists. The individuality of the soul is a unique manifestation of each individual originating from Buddha's Light. This individuality was developed through spiritual discipline undergone in a physical body on earth. Each soul has a long history of individuality, and this individualization itself is what Buddha is happy about. There are many souls that have developed in different ways, but the original nature of each soul is light. Although we are essentially the same as children of Buddha, each of us is expected to develop a unique individuality. We are such an existence that has these two contradictory aspects.

Let me delve into a more detailed explanation.

The fundamental mistake Buddhist scholars make is their misunderstanding of human existence as a temporary composite of *five aggregates*.

The five aggregates are *matter, feeling, perception, volition*, and *consciousness*. Matter or form refers to the physical body; feeling or sensation is the function of the senses; perception is the forming of an image or an idea; volition is the function of the will, which puts an idea or image into practice; and consciousness is the function of recognition or understanding.

In other words, first, there is a physical body (matter); then you feel something (feeling) and have an image or idea (perception). Next, you have the power of the will to do something to manifest the image or idea (volition), and finally you see the whole picture of what you are doing or have done (consciousness).

A human being is a temporary composite of these five factors. Except for the physical body, the remaining four are mental functions related to the heart and mind. In short, a human being is composed of a physical body and heart and mind. There is such kind of thinking.

This leads to the following idea: "A human being is temporarily made up of these five different elements—a physical body and the four mental functions—that are non-substantial in origin. This sort of being is transient and therefore impermanent—if the wind blows, it will fly away, or if burned by fire, it will disappear."

Learning this theory, many Buddhist scholars seem to have jumped to the conclusion that because a human being is a temporary composite of the five aggregates, he or she will dissolve and disappear into thin air as spirit-like energy after death.

3

Two Types of Reincarnation

The theory of the temporary composite of five aggregates is correct in a sense; it is not completely wrong. However, the question is whether it applies to life after death.

When a person dies, he or she leaves behind their physical body. However, there is also something called the astral body on the outer layer of the soul. When you die, you go back to the other world in the astral body. The astral body is what spirits "wear" when they appear as ghosts, and the five aggregates that come from the mind and body as described above are the main workings of this body. The astral body is closely connected to the sensual organs and internal organs such as the heart, intestines, and brain.

This is one of the reasons Happy Science insists that organ transplants are a questionable practice. Internal organs have their own consciousnesses and these consciousnesses constitute the astral body. When you are in the Astral Realm of the fourth dimension, you will live in this astral body.

However, when you leave there and go up to the fifth dimension or higher, you cast off the astral body and leave it behind in the fourth dimension. This astral body can sometimes get lost and appear on earth as a ghost, but usually, after some time, it is used for other purposes. As time passes, the astral body loses its human form and becomes something like old clothing. Old astral bodies left behind in the fourth dimension can be collected to be recycled as material to form the spiritual bodies of babies to be born into this world.

In the other world of the fifth dimension and higher, you will live in a true spiritual body after casting off the astral body, the part associated with your physical life. The spiritual body, which is what is left after you cast off the astral body, is not something that perishes after death. So egolessness essentially does not mean that everything perishes after death. In most cases, people continue to live in the other world after death in the form of a spiritual body, which could be called the soul, and it takes a somewhat human form. The soul reincarnates between this world and the other world. The soul continues to exist as the subject of reincarnation.

There is one more thing I must explain here. It is said that according to Shakyamuni Buddha, anyone who attains enlightenment can escape the cycle of reincarnation and will no longer need to be born on earth. Why did he make such a statement?

It is true that after death, people live on in the other world as souls in human form and are reborn on earth once every few hundred years. But in higher worlds, such as the seventh dimension and above, most souls no longer take a human form. Up to the sixth dimensional Light Realm, souls live in a human form and are reborn on earth as humans. In contrast, souls in the Bodhisattva Realm and higher are less likely to take a human form. In the Tathagata Realm, they rarely take a human form. Although they may have an image of themselves as humans, which comes from having lived their lives on earth, they usually live only as consciousnesses without form.

As they exist only as bodies of consciousnesses, they are no longer souls bound to reincarnate like ordinary humans. They become massive bodies of consciousnesses. Each consciousness has its own particular character or color such as green, blue, yellow or red, and exists only as a consciousness to carry out its functions.

At this stage, consciousnesses are no longer obliged to reincarnate time and again like ordinary human souls do; they do not have to be born into this world to undergo spiritual discipline and reap their karma. Because they exist only as bodies of consciousnesses, there is no compulsory spiritual discipline for them.

However, they sometimes choose to be born into a human body to save people on earth. Their reincarnation is determined by their own will; it is not the kind of compulsory reincarnation that ordinary human souls have to experience every several hundred years to reap their karma. It is not the type of spiritual training as if you are being tossed around in the washing machine.

Although Shakyamuni Buddha taught such a high-level concept, his disciples were unable to grasp the true meaning of his words. Many of his disciples had already concluded, "Because Buddha said that the self does not essentially exist, it must be true that human beings disappear after death." This misinterpretation on the part of the disciples caused much confusion later on.

At its worst, this misunderstanding led to the argument, "Buddhism teaches egolessness, so the soul must disappear after death." These days, about half of all Buddhist priests seem to agree with this interpretation. They say, "In Buddhism, we deny the soul. Your ego perishes when you die." If asked why they read sutras for the dead during funerals, they respond, "We are performing a service to console the bereaved family." There is a high possibility of these priests falling to hell after they die, and quite a number of scholars misunderstand the same way.

They have come to think in this way because the spiritual explanation of Buddha's teaching of egolessness was too difficult for them to understand. They conclude that because egolessness means the soul perishes after death, Buddha denied the existence of the soul.

However, what results from this misunderstanding is materialism. It denies the existence of life after death. In fact, some of the traditional Indian religions criticize Buddhism as a form of materialism in the guise of a religion. Many European religious scholars also define Buddhism as a materialistic and atheistic philosophy.

4

Parable of the Poisoned Arrow

There is another reason this interpretation was born of Buddhism.

In the Cula-Malunkyaputta Sutra, there is a dialogue between Buddha and a disciple named Malunkyaputta, who posed metaphysical questions about what happens after death and whether the universe is finite or infinite. Buddha, however, gave no reply to these questions and instead presented the famous parable of the poisoned arrow:

A man had been shot with a poisoned arrow and was on the verge of death.

When someone tried to pull out the arrow to treat him, the man said, "Wait. First, tell me who fired this arrow, where it came from, and what kind of poison it contains. I don't want to be treated without knowing the answers."

Then the person trying to treat him replied, "What are you saying? If I don't treat you, the poison will spread through your body and kill you. What is most important right now is to treat you by pulling out the arrow, wrapping the wound tightly to prevent the poison from circulating through your body, and draining the bad blood. Later, we can consider who shot the arrow, where it came from, what it's made of, and the reason you were shot. Before anything else, I must treat your wound."

This parable meant to say that metaphysical arguments and abstract discussions that are of no practical use in improving life will not help people. These sorts of arguments should be avoided until you have put your own life in order. First, you should explore the Right Mind. You should master the Eightfold Path. Then you will be freed from suffering and will enter the path to true happiness. Without doing this, there would be no point in arguing about what happens to the soul after death or whether the universe is finite or infinite.

This is what Buddha intended to say through the parable of the poisoned arrow, but because his disciples did not understand his true intention, they later explained his teaching in the following way: "Buddha didn't answer because there must be no life nor universe after death, but only this earthly world. All we have to do is live rightly in this world." This shows how difficult it is for disciples to understand their master's true intention. Please remember this well.

I think you can imagine why Buddha avoided further discussion with his disciple. Suppose someone who was living a disorderly life and whose mind was always restless came to see me and asked me the following questions:

"Master Okawa, please teach me about the human soul. How often do I reincarnate? Is there really life after death?

I've also heard that each human soul has a core spirit and branch spirits, but am I the core spirit or a branch spirit? What was I like when this universe was first created? How many hundreds of millions of years ago did I become a human?"

To someone like this, I would answer:

"Before you ask me such questions, you must first reconcile with your wife. You don't seem to be very kind to your parents, either. And you have door-key kids. They are always crying because no one is at home when they come back from school. What are you going to do about that?"

This is an example of a sermon most appropriate to a specific individual.

I am just preaching according to what the person needs most, but there are others who hear my words and take them to be universal teaching. Those who lack intelligence or flexibility of thought tend to take everything teachers say down to a T.

Buddha never denied the existence of the other world or reincarnation. Nor did he say he knew nothing about whether there is an end to the universe. But because he did not answer his disciple's metaphysical questions, people later mistook his lack of reply as negation. So you can see how difficult it is to preach the Law. People are caught up in the words they hear and fail to understand the meaning behind them.

As a result of these sorts of mistakes on the part of Buddha's disciples, a new school of Buddhism called the Zen sect was founded later on. They do not explain enlightenment in words because the students become bound by a particular explanation. For example, on hearing that there is no self, some could conclude, "Because there is no self, there is no soul, so there is no life after death." On the other hand, if the teacher says, "There is the self. Because a human being has the self, it is important to improve and develop the self," then the students might focus only on improving themselves, disregarding the importance of becoming egoless.

Please be aware that you, too, have this tendency to interpret the teachings too simplistically. All these mistakes come from a lack of understanding, which stems from ignorance, as I described in Chapter Two.

5

How to Become Truly Egoless

I have so far discussed the problems pertaining to the idea of egolessness from a spiritual point of view. Now, let me talk about the real reason Shakyamuni Buddha taught egolessness.

One of the reasons he emphasized egolessness was to teach that the cause of suffering lies mostly in attachment. Attachment means clinging to something. At the root of attachment lies the ego or self, the thought of *I* or *me*— in other words, a self-centered, biased perspective based on what is convenient for you. Most suffering is caused by a self-centered perspective or a desire.

Of the Eight Pains experienced in life, the pain of not getting what you want is the most typical of this kind of suffering. Everyone suffers from it. This pain of not getting what you want is rooted in the ego; the word *mine* derives from the thought, *I am.*

If there is no *I am*, there would be no *mine*.

You may think, "That person is *mine*," "He is *my* subordinate," "He is *my* lover," "She is *my* wife," "They are *my* children," "They are *my* parents," "This is *my* house," "This is *my* land," "This is *my* bat," "This is *my* ball," "This is *my* camera," "This is *my* purse," "This is *my* money," "This is *my* bankbook," "This is *my* business card," "This is *my* desk," "This is *my* chair," "This is *my* grave," and so on.

First, there is the thought of *I* or *me*, and this leads to the idea, "This is mine." Your sense of possession gives birth to attachment.

To abandon such attachment, you have to let go of the thought, "This is mine."

What is your true being? Your true being is a manifestation of light that came into being upon the wish of the Creator of the Universe, the Primordial Buddha. Do not forget that. When you remember the origin of your existence, you can become one with Buddha.

Going back to the teaching of egolessness, it should be re-examined from two angles. The idea of egolessness was not meant to imply that there is no such thing as the physical self. One of the essences of egolessness requires you to become one with Buddha. Unless you are selfless, you cannot become one with Buddha. If you are too concerned about yourself, Buddha's Light won't come shining into you.

The Buddhist approach to becoming one with Buddha is through self-reflection and meditation, whereas the Christian approach is through prayer to God. You can also become one with the divine through praying wholeheartedly to God. This is one way to achieve the state of egolessness.

Another way to become truly egoless is the path of altruism, or loving others.

Live for others.
Feel the pain of others as your own,
Feel the sorrow of others as your own,
And feel the joy of others as your own.
Live with a loving heart.

This is another way to become egoless.

In short, becoming one with Buddha and becoming one with other people are both teachings of egolessness. They are paths for improving and nurturing your soul.

Those who go to the hell realm in the other world after death all have some form of attachment to their ego or their possessions. Some still wander the earth as stray spirits, possessing those on earth, or they might cling to their spouse, children, or house.

Some cling to the land they owned, others to their grave. There are even those who cling to their desk at the office where they worked when they were alive. They are called earthbound spirits. In Japan, we sometimes hear of government offices where people often commit suicide. For example, suppose a high-ranking government official jumped out the window and died. Then every following year, someone working near his desk commits suicide. In such a case, there is no doubt that the officer became an earthbound spirit.

In this way, spirits of hell are bound by attachment; they are all full of attachment. And their attachment comes from *I am*. Unless they deny this ego, they won't be able to get rid of their attachment.

Heaven is an altruistic world where all the inhabitants live for the benefit of others. They live for the sake of helping others. This is the state of egolessness. They live not for themselves but for others. That is how the idea of egolessness should be understood.

6

Egolessness as the Theory of Salvation

Whether you return to heaven or to hell depends on whether you can eliminate your ego. This may sound paradoxical: the ego must be eliminated, but it must also be refined at the same time.

Spiritual discipline is something you undertake for your own benefit. It is a way of improving and developing yourself, and in this context, the ego or self may be perceived to be something that is allowed to exist. If your self-discipline is directed toward Buddha, it will lead you to become one with Buddha, and eventually you will approach the state of egolessness. Similarly, if your self-discipline is directed toward the path of altruism with the aim of saving others, you will also be led to the state of egolessness.

Devoting yourself to your own study, setting aside time for yourself, and taking care of your own health are necessary as part of your self-discipline. These attitudes may seem to increase your ego, but as long as you are moving in the direction of Buddha, an altruistic direction, you are approaching the state of egolessness.

But if your self-development results in attachment to the things of this world or to the earthly way of life, then you are on the wrong path, a path that will eventually lead you to hell.

At the beginning of this chapter, I talked about a famous Buddhist scholar. He conducted extensive research to explain Buddhist theory and even compiled a complete set of teachings. However, in the end, he could not understand the true meaning of Buddha's teachings on egolessness.

In the history of Buddhism, such confusion arose as a result of the misinterpretation by Buddha's disciples. So we could say it was inevitable that this scholar could not understand. Sadly, this is the limitation of those who have studied Buddhism from only an intellectual standpoint.

Some of you readers may also study the Truth in that way and leave behind similar mistakes for future generations. However, it would be meaningless to merely explain the teachings in an intellectual or abstract way if this does not lead to saving others. Even if some great metaphysical theory were to be expounded, if it does not contribute to people's happiness, it wouldn't mean anything.

I want you to really grasp what I have been saying and know the true meaning of the teaching of egolessness. Some may think egoless means, "There is no self, so killing yourself is no big deal." Even in the times of Shakyamuni Buddha, there were some materialists who said, "A human being is a gathering of atoms and molecules. Therefore, even if you slice a human being, it won't be murder. The blade just simply passed through the space between molecules."

Although there can be all sorts of theories about spiritual teachings, they should not be used in a way that will lead people astray or prevent them from being saved. More than half the people living on earth now are on the wrong path and are bound for hell, so the Laws must be explained in a way that will help save those who have gone astray. If you are stubborn in giving an abstract and metaphysical explanation, you will be able to save neither yourself nor others.

Please keep in mind that the purpose of disseminating the teachings is to save people.

CHAPTER FIVE

Emptiness and Causality

1

The Idea of Emptiness in Buddhism

In the previous chapter, I spoke about egolessness. You may still have difficulty understanding what egolessness really means because to have a true understanding of egolessness is almost the same as attaining enlightenment in Zen Buddhism. Since ancient times, Zen Buddhist monks have continued their disciplines to attain this enlightenment—the state of liberation from the bondage of the body and mind—as experienced by the Japanese Zen master Dogen (1200–1253), but they are rarely able to achieve it.

For this reason, I would like to continue by explaining an idea deeply connected to egolessness—the idea of emptiness or void (*sunyata* in Sanskrit).

Of the Three Dharma Seals, which are the impermanence of all things, the egolessness of all phenomena, and the perfect tranquility of nirvana, the second seal is sometimes considered to be identical with the idea, "all is empty." The egolessness of all phenomena is explained in many ways, such as "All things are non-substantial, so they are without ego or self" or "All things essentially have the same nature as Buddha," and these definitions have some connection with the idea that all things are empty.

This idea of emptiness is also very difficult to understand, but it is the very essence of Buddhism, especially Mahayana Buddhism, where it is considered to be the core within the core of all teachings.

The previous chapter and this one include concepts that are quite difficult to understand. If you could clearly understand them after reading them through only once, then that would mean you are already enlightened. These concepts are difficult to understand straightaway, and that is why there is a need for further study and spiritual discipline.

Egolessness and *emptiness* are words in the world of enlightenment. It is almost impossible for anyone to understand these concepts just intellectually—in other words, you cannot really understand them without spiritual insight or enlightenment. These concepts must be understood through enlightenment-nature. They are not something that can be grasped through intellect, reason, or sensibility. It depends on the level of insight of the individual.

Therefore, although I can explain these words in one way or another, whether or not you can grasp their true meaning depends on your own effort.

Now, I would like to first talk about emptiness. I have already explained it in the book, *The Essence of Buddha* (New York: IRH Press, 2016).

Emptiness is often compared with nothingness. These concepts are the subject of many philosophical arguments, so it may be tough to bring up each point. However, at this time, my idea regarding them is as follows:

Emptiness or void as expounded in Buddhism does not mean there is nothing, but it denotes that things change with the passage of time and therefore aren't solid or fixed substances. Things change into various forms in the flow of time, which roughly means they do not have true substance. This is how we should understand the idea of emptiness.

On the other hand, nothingness can be explained in the following way. Suppose you can stop time. All things would be static. At that time, you might ask whether or not those things actually exist. In other words, all things exist only because Buddha's Will allows them to exist. If it were not for Buddha's Will, all things would cease to exist; they would disappear. This is the concept of nothingness.

The above explanation is the difference between nothingness and emptiness.

2

The Impermanence of All Things and the Egolessness of All Phenomena

I have just explained the idea of emptiness in relation to the egolessness of all phenomena, but you might also wonder, "Perhaps the idea of emptiness has to do with the impermanence of all things." You might ask yourself, "What is the difference between the impermanence of all things and the egolessness of all phenomena? Aren't both ideas related to emptiness? They both talk about changes in the flow of time, so they must be referring to the same thing."

It seems to me that many Buddhist scholars confuse these two ideas. When I read a book by a well-known Japanese Buddhist leader, I found that he has mistaken these ideas as one for the other. Since he can get by with that, I presume even religious professionals have difficulty understanding these ideas.

How can we explain them in the right way?

The egolessness of all phenomena cannot be explained without taking the Spirit World into consideration. It is impossible to explain this idea within the scope of our world alone without taking into consideration the cycles of life between this world and the next, or the materialization of spiritual beings and the dematerialization of earthly beings between this world and the Spirit World.

The impermanence of all things, however, can be discussed without taking the existence of the other world into consideration. All things in this world change moment by moment: they go through birth, growth, and maturity, and they eventually decay and disappear. Seeds that are sown will grow, flower, wither, and finally go back to the earth. Likewise, human beings are born as babies, grow up as children, become adults and work, grow old and have a hunched back, and die.

In this way, everything in this world goes through the cycle of birth, growth, decline, and death, so it is easy for anyone to see that all things are impermanent in this world.

However, to see the impermanence of all things in the truest sense, you also need to consider the spiritual point of view. From the standpoint of the other world, it becomes more obvious that all things in this world are transient and ephemeral; there is nothing firm and stable.

On the other hand, the egolessness of all phenomena depicts cycles on a far greater scale.

To explain this in relation to time, the following illustration may be helpful. Suppose there is an enormous waterwheel. As the waterwheel slowly turns, the paddles dip into the stream, push the water, and come up again, one after another.

In this case, the impermanence of all things refers mainly to the part of the wheel going under the water—that is, the part symbolizing the Phenomenal World—whereas the egolessness of all phenomena refers to the entire waterwheel. I think it is easier to understand if you think in this way.

However, this explanation alone is not enough. It is just an example purely in relation to time. The impermanence of all things describes phenomena that occur within a certain period of time in this world. On the other hand, the egolessness of all phenomena encompasses a greater flow of time.

3

Emptiness—
(1) The Cycle between
This World and the Spirit World

Now, let me explain how the idea of emptiness is connected to the idea of the egolessness of all phenomena from three different perspectives.

First, emptiness can be explained in terms of the relationship between this world and the other world.

Suppose you are watching a movie in a movie theater. You see many scenes, one after another, on the two-dimensional screen. For example, in the movie *Back to the Future Part III*, there is a scene where the hero travels back to the past in a time machine and is chased by Native Americans, like a cowboy in a Western movie.

As you watch the movie, you feel as if you are actually experiencing the situation, breathlessly cheering him on. However, what appears on the screen is just a video image and not a real person. What appears are simply pictures on a film. Nevertheless, you cannot help identifying with the hero and feeling as if the scenes were real.

The way people in this world appear to the eyes of spirits in the other world is very similar. If seen from the other world, or the Real World, life in this world seems like a temporary dream or illusion.

Human beings live in a physical body, struggle with worries, suffer on and on, and feel joy and sorrow with all their heart over the course of a lifetime. But once their life on earth is over and they go backstage, they realize that what they experienced was rather like a play. You may have played the role of a king, a princess, a soldier, or a Native American; everyone plays their part seriously, but after the play is over, they return backstage, where those who were killed come back to life with a sigh of relief.

In this way, our lives are shown like plays or movies. What we experience is not real; it is temporary. That is the earthly world.

At present, your guardian spirit is watching you from the other world. A part of you that resides in the other world is watching you act in this world. You appear to them as if you are projected onto a screen and they are cheering you on with all their might.

Needless to say, in the past, cheering on the actors in the movie on-screen did not actually reach the actors, but nowadays, satellite broadcasting allows words of encouragement spoken in some far, distant place to be instantaneously transmitted to the actors. Telephones also make it possible for two parties at distant locations to communicate with each other. The relationship between this world and the Spirit World could be described as something like this.

When you go back to the other world after spending decades performing spiritual training on earth, usually, your life in this world will be played back to you on a screen. In some cases, your life might be played to you in a mirror. In as little as an hour, your entire life in this world will be shown before you as if you are watching a movie. It will be as if you are being asked, "That was your life. What did you think of it? Did you think the movie was interesting? Was it well made or not?" The movie will be stored deep in your soul as a memory of your past life, and you can watch it whenever you want.

That is how we are seen from the Spirit World. We go back and forth between this world and the other world. We live in a physical body, but this body is rather like a stuffed doll. It is just like the costume an actor puts on when he plays a part on the stage. It is the role you are playing, not the essential nature of your being. When you return backstage, your ordinary life resumes, and this ordinary life is your spiritual life in the other world.

Basically, what you think to be true in this world is not true. It is only temporary, and your true life is the life after you return backstage. However, you cannot entirely say that only the life during your time backstage is true. Even after you return backstage, you sometimes come back on stage and play another part; this time, you may act the part of a Native American, act like a peacock, or maybe even fly in the sky. You can have such experiences.

So you can act properly and be a movie star when you are on stage, but once you come backstage, you can return to living a normal life. And not only do you remain backstage, you can also come back on stage. This is what is meant by the Buddhist expression: *Matter is void, void is matter.*

Here, *matter* means material objects, a physical body, or an earthly existence. This matter or earthly existence is an actor in a drama; on returning backstage, the actor returns to their usual life. This is what is meant by *matter is void*. But after living an ordinary life for some time, the actor reappears on the stage to play a different part. This is, *void is matter*. So *matter is void* and *void is matter* are both true.

Therefore, the idea of emptiness could first be understood as a concept explaining the cycle between this world and the Spirit World.

4

Emptiness—
(2) Buddha's Light and Materialization

Now, let me move on to the second explanation regarding emptiness.

Emptiness is not just about the cycle between this world and the other world in the flow of time. Everything you can see in this world is a physical manifestation of the unseen, and conversely, the visible can also transform into the invisible. This transformation doesn't necessarily occur with the passage of time as mentioned in the previous section. Such a phenomenon is called materialization.

Believers of Happy Science have seen gold dust appearing on their palms or on their faces or shoulders. There are also times when such gold dust grows into something bigger, like a flake.

We are not using alchemy; gold dust comes out of nowhere. Once you actually experience materialization, you will know that material things can appear out of thin air, though they may not be natural or human-made objects.

Miracles usually happen in the same way. For example, when Moses and the Israelites were all hungry and wandering in the wilderness after escaping from Egypt, as described in the Book of Exodus, they ate food called *manna* that appeared out of thin air and their hunger was satisfied. There is such a story, and you can understand that materialization really does occur.

Gold dust really materializes out of nowhere; it is real gold and can be examined under a microscope. But usually, the gold dust disappears in about a week, like snow. Although at one time it appears as gold, it eventually disappears. From this, we can see that material objects in this world can be produced by spiritual energy.

The same could be said of illness. Cancer is an example of a foreign substance that grows in the body as a result of negative spiritual effect.

However, we often hear stories of cancer disappearing as a result of faith. I have even heard of a large stomach tumor that disappeared in a short period of time. A cancerous tumor had been detected in a patient's stomach, but an X-ray showed no trace of it. This could be another way of explaining *Matter is void, void is matter*.

It means, the *visible* can come from the *invisible*, and what is visible at the current moment can vanish into the world of the invisible. Illnesses appear and disappear under the same phenomenon. Unlike the reincarnation cycle between this world and the other, which includes an earthly life of several decades, materialization and dematerialization occur in an instant. This, too, could be an explanation of *Matter is void, void is matter*.

Modern physics has reported many similar cases. For example, physicists often say elementary particles suddenly appear and disappear like ghosts, and they seem to have difficulty understanding this. The elementary particles behave like light, particles, and waves; like ghosts, they can pass through walls.

I presume that as modern physics advances further, the theory of emptiness described here will be explained scientifically.

In this section, I have used the cases of gold dust and illness as examples. On a larger scale, theoretically, these cases can be explained according to the Physics of Buddha's Light, as described in Chapter One of *The Golden Laws* (Tokyo, HS Press, 2015).

When Buddha's Light remains in a spiritual state, it exists in the Real World, but when its wavelength becomes less refined and heavier, it materializes in this world.

Although you can say that the body and spirit are two separate things, they can also be considered one and the same.

The spiritual body and physical body are different when seen from an earthly standpoint, but according to the Physics of Buddha's Light, all things are essentially made from Buddha's Light. The spiritual body is made of Buddha's Light. When the spiritual body becomes much heavier, to the point of being able to withstand great pressure, like an object at the bottom of the sea, it transforms into matter.

Simply put, we who exist in this material world are like crabs crawling at the bottom of the deep sea. Although crabs live under tons of pressure, they are not destroyed by it. We are similar in that our physical body is rather like the shell of a crab. We were made to withstand such pressure.

In this way, dualism can explain that the spirit and the physical body are different things, but at the same time, are made from the same element. This is the second explanation regarding emptiness.

5

Emptiness——
(3) As Seen in the Law of Causality

The third way of explaining the idea of emptiness is using the law of causality or the law of cause and effect.

This explanation is also often used in traditional Buddhism. Behind this explanation is the idea that our true being, or what is real, is unchangeable and perpetually exists without undergoing any transformation. What continues to exist eternally, is what is real.

Looking at the things of this world, however, we can see that nothing is truly substantial. Consider a clock, for example. It may look as if it actually exists, but there must have been a process by which it was made before it came into being. The metallic parts were probably made of metal that came from a mine in another country. First, the metal was refined and brought into this country; then it was melted down and molded into the form of a clock.

Besides manufacturing the parts of the clock, there are other processes involving the assembly of the parts that make up the mechanism of the clock. There is also a process that goes into making the glass parts and the hands of the clock. Special techniques are used to make the clock face. Paint is applied to the face. Now, how was this paint made?

Numbers are printed on the face, but who invented these numbers? Someone in an ancient civilization must have invented mathematics. The mechanism of the clock was also invented and actually made into a tangible form by someone. To mass-produce clocks, you need to have factories and the manpower of tons of workers. So it seems as though we are looking at a clock as a product of the accumulation of many processes.

If a clock were real, it would have existed from ancient times, but in reality, that is not true. It is clear that a clock exists due to the accumulation of invisible processes.

So the answer to the question of whether or not a clock really exists or whether it is truly substantial is, "No, it is not." It only appears as a clock at this moment because there were a number of different factors involved in making it, such as human labor, materials, and parts. It probably won't exist a hundred years from now. It will stop working, be disassembled into pieces, and be discarded at some point. It may be turned into something utterly different or perhaps decomposed back into the soil. In a hundred years' time, there may be no trace of it.

Similar to the idea of the impermanence of all things, which I have previously discussed, you can see that all things in this world are non-substantial. If they were substantial, they must be unchangeable, but the truth is that they are not. All things come into being as a result of the accumulation of many invisible factors. Objects appear to exist now, but this is like passing a point in time. When a bullet train passes a small countryside station, someone at the station can take a photo of it, but even if they want to take another shot a moment later, the train would be gone. In the same way, things in this world appear to exist at this moment, but they do not actually exist if viewed from the perspective of the longer flow of time. This is a way of seeing things from the perspective of the law of causality.

What is causality? In principle, the law of causality can be explained as a chain of cause and effect. After there is a cause, there is an effect, so the effect depends on the cause. In this chain of cause and effect, however, there is always a cause and a condition before the effect.

Let me explain this using water as an example. Water, with the formula H_2O, is a compound made up of hydrogen and oxygen, but a simple mixture of these two gases will not produce water. You need to contain the gases in a test tube and heat them with a burner until they explode to form water. The combustion instantly turns the gases into liquid. In this case, hydrogen and oxygen are the cause, combustion is the condition, and water is the effect.

The same could be said of plants. Seeds do not instantly grow into flowers. First, the seeds need to be sown; then they need to be given enough water, nutrients, and sunlight before they can grow and blossom into flowers.

Cause and condition are both necessary to obtain a result. You shouldn't think that a result will appear instantly just because there is a cause. The condition must be added.

In the case of a human being, the condition corresponds to spiritual discipline. Everyone has Buddha-nature, or the nature of tathagata, within them. In the Lankavatara Sutra, it is also called the *storehouse consciousness* (alaya-consciousness). *The Awakening of Faith in Mahayana*, translated by Paramartha, describes it as the part of *ariya-consciousness* that is devoid of ignorance (because the ariya-consciousness is considered a combination of true and delusory consciousnesses). Other terms for Buddha-nature include *tathagata-garbha*, *innate pure mind* or *amala-consciousness* (untainted consciousness in the theory of nine consciousnesses), and *true thusness*. Although you have Buddha-nature within you, you won't attain buddhahood without making an effort to develop yourself spiritually. This is also an application of the law of causality.

6

Spiritual Discipline and Transformation through Permeation

Regrettably, people often misunderstand this point; some Buddhists seem to believe that because all people have the same essential nature as Buddha, all are equal and so everyone must be a buddha. This misunderstanding completely ignores the process of spiritual discipline. Such an understanding is tantamount to saying that if there is a seed, the flower has already bloomed.

However, that is not true. Although everyone has Buddha-nature within them, there must be certain conditions to make it bloom. Just as there are conditions for flowers to bloom, humans must also undergo spiritual discipline to attain buddhahood.

Spiritual discipline involves learning the Truth and practicing the teachings. You must also keep disciplining your mind. Only after you have gone through these practices can you taste the fruit called enlightenment. Enlightenment can be attained as the result of you refining the nature of tathagata, or the Buddha-nature. And by attaining enlightenment, you become a buddha.

The process of spiritual discipline toward enlightenment is called "learnings that permeate the soul." Similar to the deep, rich flavor of smoked salmon, what you learn over time will seep deep into you until it becomes habitual. This is known as the doctrine of permeation.

Everything you learn during the decades of your spiritual training on earth permeates into you, and some lessons are engraved deep into your soul. When they reach the part of the subconscious known as alaya-consciousness[3], they will become part of the karma that you take with you when you are reborn the next time. The lessons that permeate your soul become karma; in other words, they appear as the tendencies of your soul. This process of forming the tendency of the soul is called permeation.

This is also called the theory of transformation through permeation. It means that the result comes after the lessons seep in and various conditions are added. This explanation covers most of Buddha's teaching on causality.

To sum up, the accumulation of many invisible factors yields a result, and this result in turn becomes the cause of the next event. In this way, all things in this world are formed as a consequence of a series of cause and effect. The existence of one thing is dependent on another, so it can be said that they are not substantial; therefore, they are empty.

This is the theory underlying the idea of emptiness. All things are dependent on other things, and in Buddhism, this is called "the nature of dependence." If something is dependent on another, it cannot be substantial; something that depends on another to exist is not substantial. This is the thinking behind traditional Buddhist studies.

In this chapter, I have discussed emptiness in three ways. First, it was explained in relation to the cycle between this world and the Spirit World. Second, the materialization of spiritual energy into this world and the dematerialization of matter into the Spirit World were discussed. Finally, emptiness was explained in connection with the law of causality, making it clear that things that depend on other things are non-substantial; they did not originally exist.

There are no traditional writings on Buddhism that explain emptiness with this much clarity, so you can say this explanation is originally made by Happy Science.

Some thinkers simply take emptiness to be an attitude of mental detachment. Either way, I will continue to explain ideas like emptiness and causality in further detail.

CHAPTER SIX

Karma and Reincarnation

1

Karma and Religion

In this chapter, I will describe the system of reincarnation in relation to the theory of the 12-fold chain of causality, which is an extension of the law of causality described in the last chapter. You may have heard the word *karma* before, but do you know what it really means? Karma is actually the tendencies that you have developed in your mind as you lived on earth, from birth until death. Because these are tendencies, once they are formed, you base your thoughts and actions on them. Although the tendencies were born from you, once they are formed, they begin to influence your thoughts and actions. That is karma.

By analyzing karma in different ways, religion teaches people the truth about human beings and a true way to live. Religion differs from ethics in that it teaches people how to live in relation to the next life. The true purpose of religion is to teach people to follow the right way of life while explaining the relationship between this life and the next. You cannot learn this from philosophy, ethics, or medical science. Religion is essentially a very general field, a comprehensive study of human beings, which allows people to learn how to live in harmony with all other beings in this vast world.

To those who have studied Buddhism, the idea of the 12-fold chain of causality may be familiar, but many people seem to have difficulty remembering all the 12 elements in this formula. This idea of 12 links was not actually one of Shakyamuni Buddha's original teachings but came from some of his disciples who further studied the law of causality and broke it down into 12 elements.

2

The Three Passages—
Delusion, Karma, and Suffering

The law of cause and effect that Shakyamuni Buddha discovered under the bodhi tree is none other than the interrelation of three elements in life—delusion, karma, and suffering—which in Buddhism are known as the Three Passages. *Delusion* here refers to the Three Poisons of the Mind, which are greed, anger, and foolishness, as explained in Chapter Two. These are the major causes of human delusion.

As these three poisons take over your life, your mind develops particular tendencies; this is called *karma*. Delusion forms karma, be it good or bad. Karma itself is value-neutral and includes good tendencies such as kindness to others.

However, when people are left to themselves, they tend to head in the wrong direction. It wouldn't be such a big problem if people could head in the right direction by themselves. This is why there is a need for religion. So the word *karma*, in many cases, has negative connotations.

You create your karma based on the Three Poisons of the Mind, and this leads to *suffering*. You will experience suffering even while you are alive, of course. For example, if you lead a dissipated life in your younger days, you will have to pay for it in your middle age and twilight years.

Excessive eating and drinking in your youth will naturally lead to a decline in your health in later years. If you did not study diligently in your younger years, you might not be able to succeed in your career. If you have caused a lot of trouble at home, what will await you in your final years will be loneliness and misery.

In this way, the phenomenon of suffering occurs in your present life, but the adverse effects can also be carried over to your next life on earth. The karma you developed in this life will lead to your suffering in the Three Realms of transmigration.

In Buddhism, the Three Realms are the Realm of Desire, the Realm of Form, and the Realm of Formlessness. The Realm of Desire is a world in which people repeatedly reincarnate as a result of human desires. The Realm of Form is a world where the inhabitants are more detached from human desires and more spiritually advanced, whereas the Realm of Formlessness is a place where the inhabitants are free of any human attributes—in other words, a world of brahmas or tathagatas.

Those who live in the Realm of Desire still cling to earthly life. Those who deeply understand the importance of spirituality inhabit the Realm of Form, which extends from the upper level of the sixth dimension to the seventh dimension. The Realm of Formlessness is where high spirits of the eighth dimension and above reside, conscious of their own spiritual nature as brahmas or tathagatas. The afterlife is mainly divided into these three different realms, and it is said that those in the Realm of Desire repeatedly reincarnate between this world and the so-called six paths or six realms of existence—namely, the realm of hell, the realm of hungry ghosts, the realm of animals, the realm of asura (spirits who are fond of fighting), the human realm, and the realm of deities.

When these people are born again, they often ask themselves, "Why should I lead such a miserable life?" "Why was I born into such a lowly family?" "Why was I born with this sort of destiny?" They tend to blame heaven, other people, or their parents.

To answer these questions, the following new teaching was given: "It is you, yourself, who is to blame. The reason you suffer these conditions now is because of the way you lived your past life, which led to your present life. So you should not blame other people or your environment for your unhappiness, let alone God or Buddha."

The next life will truly come, and regardless of whether your present life is full of suffering, you will certainly have the next life. Therefore, thinking of the life to come, you have to carefully examine your present state, and if you are suffering now, you must try to eliminate the cause and prevent yourself from suffering in the next life.

Otherwise, you will lose the chance to eliminate the causes. Eliminate the root of misfortune while you can in this lifetime. Eliminate the source of your suffering to come in the next life.

This is what Shakyamuni Buddha taught.

3

The Five-Fold Chain and the 10-Fold Chain of Causality

A more developed form of the theory of the Three Passages, which comprises delusion, karma, and suffering, is the theory of the five-fold chain of causality. It explains the origin of suffering by breaking it down into five factors. This theory was already known in Shakyamuni's time.

Of the five links, first comes *tanha* or craving. It is a state of thirst or hunger where you cannot help but want more and more. It is the feeling you have when you skip breakfast and lunch—you would eat dinner like a wild animal. The obsessive desire for something is *tanha*.

Next comes *grasping*, which is attachment to one particular thing and how it never leaves your mind.

These first two links create *existence*, or the state of living in delusion, which could also be called the tendency of the soul.

As a result, there comes *birth* into the next life; consequently, there is the suffering of *aging and death*.

In this theory, the Three Passages have been expanded to five factors.

To help you understand it better, let me take appetite as an example.

In this world, some people seem to live solely for the pursuit of eating. They find eating the greatest pleasure in life and are attached to the deliciousness of the food, always thinking about what kind of food they will have next—French, Chinese, etc. In this case, an attachment to food has been imprinted in their souls.

When they go back to the other world after death, they feel dissatisfied because they cannot actually eat. Although they can feel as if they are eating in the other world, it is much different from the pleasures of eating that they enjoyed on earth, so they are keen to come back to earth to once again enjoy eating good food. So they are reborn into this world and live for several decades, always wanting to eat. Then, they get old and eventually die in a state of suffering. These people repeat this process again and again, living a life very close to that of an animal.

As another example, let us consider sensual desire. This kind of craving is experienced when one is struck by the beauty of the opposite sex, when they are no longer able to contain themselves, which then results in grasping (attachment), causing the person to become deeply involved in a relationship. He or she begins to think that sensual pleasure is the greatest joy in this world, just like the appetite for food in the example I gave earlier; they believe that there is no greater happiness than having relations with the opposite sex. Then, these thoughts become fixed and imprinted in the person's soul. It means the thoughts clearly become an existence.

When these people lose their physical bodies and go back to the other world, they miss their physical bodies very much and desperately wish to be reborn. They crave to be reborn and enjoy their life with the opposite sex, believing that paradise exists on earth. Then, after being reborn and living another life of indulgence in sensual pleasures, they suffer from aging and death again.

Shakyamuni Buddha talked about this cycle of rebirth in the world of delusion while he was alive.

After his death, however, his disciples analyzed the idea of five links further and developed the 10-fold chain of causality.

Here, I would like to explain the term *causality*. Causality is a concept that explains how things occur in relation to time. It implies a relationship between cause and effect; there is always a cause and a condition (indirect cause) that give birth to something. The term causality implies that things are unceasingly forming and transforming in the flow of time.

Now, let me explain the 10-fold chain of causality. This theory omits the first two elements, *ignorance* and, *action*, of the 12-fold chain of causality and begins from the idea concerning rebirth. It starts with *consciousness*, which means your wish to be born into this world, then *name-and-form* or the physical formation of an embryo, followed by the arising of the *six sensory organs*—the eyes, ears, nose, tongue, body, and mind. Then *contact*, or the sense of touch, such as that through your hands and feet. Next is *feeling*. As a consequence of *feeling*, *craving* arises for the things one likes, followed by *grasping* or attachment to the things one wants. Finally, the soul develops its tendency outputted as *existence*. This leads to *birth*, or rebirth into the next life, and eventually to *aging and death*. These 10 factors are called the 10-fold chain of causality.

You may wonder why it is necessary to explain the process of rebirth by including the physical formation of the embryo. In India, in Shakyamuni's time, the study of anatomy was highly advanced, and an autopsy was often performed to study the internal organs of the human body. In those days, there was no clear line between medicine and Buddhist studies; both shared the same attitude toward research into human life.

The question of why human beings are born and where they will go after death was one of the great themes, and the process of birth was a matter of great interest to the majority of people. So research was done to find a solution. It seems this allowed the medical knowledge back then to be incorporated into the Buddhist theory of 10 links.

However, there is a problem with this theory, which I will explain in the next section dealing with the 12-fold chain of causality.

Figure 1

Causality			Cause and effect doubled over three lives		
The 12-fold chain of causality	ignorance	= craving and grasping		cause	past life
	action	= existence			
The 10-fold chain of causality	consciousness	= birth		effect	present life
	name-and-form	= aging and death			
	six sensory organs				
	contact				
	feeling				
The 5-fold chain of causality	craving	= ignorance		cause	
	grasping				
	existence	= action			
	birth	= consciousness		effect	future life
	aging and death	= name-and-form, six sensory organs, contact and feeling			

4

Reincarnation in Relation to the 12-Fold Chain of Causality

In the 12-fold chain of causality (see Figure 1), first comes *ignorance*, which is delusion derived mainly from the Three Poisons of the Mind: greed, anger, and foolishness. *Action* arises based on this delusion, and this action becomes karma. As this karma is imprinted in the depths of the soul, *consciousness* is developed, constituting the subject of the soul to be born in the next life.

When the consciousness of the soul that is to be reborn enters the physical body, it is called *name-and-form*. This term is a direct translation of the original Sanskrit term and is now commonly used, but its meaning is not clear. The original meaning of name-and-form was "spirit and physical body" or "mind and body."

Here, however, lies a problem. The theory states that consciousness first dwells in the body of an embryo to become name-and-form; then it develops the *six sensory organs*—the eyes, ears, nose, tongue, body, and mind. According to the concept of rebirth in those days, a baby's soul was thought to enter its mother's womb at the moment of conception, when the sperm fertilized the egg.

It sounds quite logical. The consciousness of a soul enters the mother's womb at the time of conception, and gradually, the physical body begins to form with the consciousness in it, followed by the development of the six sensory organs and then the arising of *contact* and, finally, *feeling*.

But my studies indicate that the soul actually enters the embryo around the ninth week or the beginning of the third month of pregnancy. Around the fourth week, the embryo is shaped like an animal, although it has something that looks like arms, legs, and a head. It is in about the eighth week of pregnancy that the embryo begins to clearly look like a human as its eyes, ears, nose, and mouth are formed. Then, around the ninth week, the soul actually enters the body. That was the case with my son. Before that, the embryo has no soul in it. Even so, it is alive.

This is probably because by around the eighth week of pregnancy, the life energies of the sperm and egg, plus that of the mother, combine to create the raw material or elements of the astral body that fits to the shape of the baby's body. In short, during the first eight weeks, some kind of consciousness that causes the physical organs to function seems to be created. It is in this period that the basis of the infant's astral body is formed, and it is only after the human shape of the baby has formed that the soul enters it. This is what I discovered.

Based on that, the theories of the 10-fold chain and 12-fold chain of causality are not very convincing. The theories say that humans are born from consciousness—a soul's consciousness enters the embryo at the time of fertilization, then the embryo develops a mind and body, and eventually it develops the six sensory organs. But in reality, at the stage of name-and-form, the consciousness of the soul is still waiting to come in from the other world, and in the mother's womb, there is only a form of flesh, an animal-like embryo.

So the term *name-and-form*, meaning spirit and physical body or mind and body, is not appropriate. The term *physical formation* is closer to the true meaning.

Because the term physical formation is not used in Buddhist studies, I don't recommend you use it. The fact is that the soul has not yet entered the body at this stage.

Next, the six sensory organs develop around the eighth or ninth week of pregnancy, when the baby's features and limbs become more distinct. The soul enters the body at this point, and it begins to take control of the embryo as a human being.

In my explanation, all the stages up to the development of the six sensory organs are relevant to the period before birth, and all the stages after are relevant to the period after birth. The stage after the development of the six sensory organs, or contact, corresponds to the period from birth until two or three years of age. After that is feeling, when sensibilities tremendously develop. This extends to the age of establishing self-awareness.

However, some scholars explain that all the stages up to feeling take place in the mother's womb. They claim that the unborn baby in the mother's womb can touch and feel. Although it is possible to assert this, there is not much point in dividing the period in the mother's womb into so many stages.

After being born into this world, the baby begins to touch and feel things and develops perceptions. Before long, it begins to become conscious of likes and dislikes. This is *craving*. It becomes particularly evident at the stage of youth, around 12–25 years of age, when one clearly feels the pleasure of having what one likes and knowing what one wants, and this is the time when one's sensual desires begin to burn.

Then, the period of attachment begins after one becomes an adult. This is the stage of *grasping*, where people become bound by all sorts of attachments to the things of this world. This stage lasts from about 25 to 50 years of age.

At around 50 years of age, the fixed tendencies of the soul, or *existence* in the theory of 10 or 12 links, are formed. Many of you may feel discouraged to hear this. Usually, at the age of 10, how you will grow up or how your next life on earth will be, would not be determined yet. At 20, this is still unknown. At 30, although the tendencies of your soul, your potential, and your ability have become more clearly visible, they are not yet fixed, so your next life is not yet fixed.

But if you have already reached 50, the evaluation of your present life is more or less determined according to your abilities and career in this lifetime, so you will be held 80 percent responsible for the way in which you have lived your life. So at the age of 50, only 20 percent remain undecided about your prospective next life. But before long, the time will come when your coffin is sealed and you will have to face the facts of your life, which will be shown on a screen in the Real World. Then, you will have to experience birth, aging, and death in the next life, which will again be full of illness, anxiety, sorrow, worries, and suffering.

Moreover, there is a theory in which the 12-fold chain of causality is further classified in the following way: "*Ignorance* and *action* in the previous life are the cause of *consciousness*, *name-and-form*, *six sensory organs*, *contact*, and *feeling* in the present life. The *craving*, *grasping*, and *existence* that are newly created during life on earth, which could also be considered *ignorance* and *action* in the present life, become the cause of *birth* and *aging and death* in the next life. There are two pairs of cause and effect." This theory shows that cause and effect are doubled by the 12-fold chain of causality through three lives: the past, the present, and the future. So this is sometimes called the theory of "cause and effect doubled over three lives." Because many of Buddha's disciples were clever philosophers, they classified these 12 links in a rather complicated fashion. It would be easier to understand if we could stick to the Three Passages. People can easily understand them if they are explained as delusion, karma, and suffering. But when it comes to the 12-fold chain of causality, it becomes difficult to study and learn them by heart.

5

The Soul's Journey through
the Past, Present, and Future

There is yet another problem with the theory of the 12-fold chain of causality. The theory, as described in the last section, is a way of seeing the chain of cause and effect operating in forward order, as follows:

Because there is *ignorance*, there arises *action*;
Because there is *action*, there arises *consciousness*;
Because there is *consciousness*, there arises *name-and-form*;
(...) Because there is *birth*, there arise *aging and death*.

This method of explanation is called the positive or direct view of causality in the flow of time.

On the contrary, there is also a way of explaining the theory through negation:

Without *ignorance*, there would be no *action* based on it;
Without *action*, there would be no *consciousness* or tendencies of the soul;
Without *consciousness*, there would be no *name-and-form*;
Without *name-and-form*, there would be no *six sensory organs*;

(...) Without *grasping*, there would be no *existence*;

Without *existence*, there would be no *birth* or *aging and death* in the next life.

This method of explanation is called the reverse view of causality through elimination. Some explain this in a different way, reflecting from the last factor: aging and death arise as a result of birth; birth arises as a result of existence; action arises as a result of ignorance; and so on.

It is said that when Shakyamuni Buddha attained his great enlightenment, he meditated on the 12-fold chain of causality in the forward and reversed order like this:

"Human beings are reborn in the following way. First, there is *ignorance*, and because of this there is *action*, (...) in consequence there is *birth*, then *aging and death*. This is the system of reincarnation. So if *ignorance* were eliminated, all the other factors would naturally vanish." Though some books actually state this, it seems too simplistic and somewhat difficult to accept.

Although it sounds quite logical, this discussion leads to the conclusion that when one has attained enlightenment and eliminated *ignorance*, all consequent factors will disappear. There will be no *birth*, no *aging and death* in the next life. In this case, if ignorance were to be eliminated, there would be no action and thus no consciousness, so it seems that even the soul would disappear. Therefore, it would mean that enlightenment leads to the disappearance of the self. If this were the case, there would be no reason to attain enlightenment.

It is clear that the above explanation was constructed by disciples who simply liked formal logic. The result of spiritual discipline should not be the disappearance of everything.

If, instead, the logic said that those who attained enlightenment remain while those who did not disappear, then it would make more sense. In Christianity, for example, people believe that those who have faith in Christ will be given eternal life, whereas the faithless will burn in the fires of hell. Although this is not exactly what happens, it is quite reasonable.

But the theory of eliminating spiritual ignorance, if misunderstood, would lead to the conclusion that those who attained enlightenment would disappear while those who did not would continue to be reborn. This creates problems. So you should consider this idea illogical.

On the other hand, some may insist it is impossible to eliminate ignorance in the first place. Of course, it is true to say that no one can completely eliminate ignorance, but you should not think like this. Rather, you should take causality to be a theory that admits that eliminating ignorance would lead to the elimination of living in delusion and, thus, the elimination of reincarnation in delusion. It is right to think that the elimination of ignorance would lead to the extinction of the misery of cycles of reincarnation, of people forgetting that the original home of their soul is the Spirit World, and instead wanting to come back to earth again and again on account of their lust or their desire for food, as previously described.

You can see a lot of characteristics of Buddhism in my explanation of the 12-fold chain of causality. While considering the soul's journey through past, present, and future lives, this theory incorporates medical knowledge, which shows how Buddhism has a tendency to take a scientific approach—a tendency to explore the cause of things deeply and try to explain things logically and reasonably.

Although the 10-fold chain of causality and 12-fold chain of causality are not actual teachings of Shakyamuni Buddha, the analytical approach and the pursuit of a logical train of thought seen in these theories are obviously based on Buddha's way of thinking. Buddhism uses this sort of approach in the pursuit of answers to every question, so you could say that even from today's perspective, Buddhism is a religion that demonstrates a logical and scientific way of thinking.

Compared with Shakyamuni's Buddhism, however, modern Buddhism seems to have become more like a set of traditional rituals and customs; it does not seem to use a logical, scientific, or medical approach to pursue things.

In any case, it is very important for us to think about life from the perspective of the chain of cause and effect. This concept is fundamental to Buddhism.

Then, what is the message I should convey to you from the chapter titled, "Karma and Reincarnation"?

All human beings reincarnate again and again, and when you think about yourself, you should not only think about the present in the current flow of time. You also have to think about your past life and future life. You need to think about how your present life will affect your life after death and your next life on this earth.

While considering your present life, perhaps you could give yourself a score.

Suppose the maximum score is 100 points. If you were to evaluate your present life, what score would you give yourself—perhaps 90, 70, 50, or 10 points? Whatever it may be, should you just be complaining about it?

If the score for your present life is low, the cause is probably to be found in your past life. So if you continue living as you are now without making any changes, your bad karma will be carried over into the next life and you will have to face the same kind of problems in that life, too. Therefore, you need to make every possible effort, in the conditions you have been given, to find the highest possible enlightenment you can attain in the present life.

Doing so will lead to your happiness in the next life. Of course, happiness in the next life can also mean the happiness you will enjoy in heaven after leaving this world as well as the happiness of the life you will have the next time you are born.

The theory of karma and reincarnation teaches you about happiness from a longer span and a broader perspective.

6

Reincarnation and the Concept of Soul Siblings

The teachings on reincarnation in Happy Science include the concept of soul siblings, or a soul group consisting of a core spirit and some branch spirits, which does not appear in traditional Buddhism. Although some Buddhist sutras contain the story of the seven Buddhas of the past, explaining Shakyamuni Buddha's past lives, it could be said that the precise system of reincarnation has been left obscure. But now, I teach that there are brother and sister souls.

In general, reincarnation has been understood as the process whereby an individual soul is born into this world again and again, but in principle, every human being is actually part of a group of six souls—one core spirit and five branch spirits—who take turns to be born into this world.

So it is necessary to think about the spiritual discipline that includes the element of the entire soul group. This means that the life of one soul living on earth affects the happiness of the other brother or sister souls. The way one soul has lived and the results of that life will affect the life plan of the next brother or sister soul to be born into this world.

Take the example of a physical body; it has organs such as the heart, liver, pancreas, and kidneys—none of these organs function under the control of the will of the individual. If you were to count your heartbeat, I'm sure you would become so bothered that you wouldn't be able to sleep at night. Nevertheless, the heart continues to live regardless of your own will. Therefore, living things with their own will, which do not listen to our will, also live inside our bodies. We exist as a composite of many such organs, and the same holds true for soul siblings.

I'm sure no one would feel odd about how the heart continues to work inside our body regardless of our will. No one would object to how our lungs breathe by themselves and how our kidneys filter urine on their own. They go on living without being told to do so and coexist even then.

The brother and sister souls of a person constitute one big soul, although they seem to live separate lives, just like the internal organs. The core spirit can be compared to the brain; its spiritual awareness is the highest of the soul group, and it determines the development of the whole soul group.

Thus, if one of the soul siblings falls to hell, it would feel as if part of the physical body became sick. It would be like having sickness or disorder in the eyes, the nose, the heart, or the kidneys. When a part of the body becomes sick, the whole body suffers.

If your brain fails, you wouldn't be able to undergo spiritual training on earth. So as you can see, because the core spirit plays a very important role, it rarely falls to hell. It is usually a branch spirit who falls.

When part of the soul siblings is in hell, the whole soul group goes through a hard time. But just as a sick person can continue to live, the other soul siblings continue to live and be active, though the total energy of the group considerably drops.

And just as you would want to cure the sick part of your body as quickly as possible, other souls in the group strive in different ways to pull up the fallen soul.

I do feel it is necessary to expand on the concept of reincarnation from the perspective of soul siblings at a later time. Nonetheless, in this chapter, I explained the fundamental principle of karma and reincarnation in line with Buddhist theory. I hope you will deepen your understanding through this chapter.

Afterword for Part One

The Truth that I teach at Happy Science covers a wide range of topics. There is a tremendous volume of teachings, but at the center of all of these lies the spirit of Buddhism as a backbone. This is the essential spirit of Buddha that transcends the differences between sects and schools and between Hinayana and Mahayana.

Buddhist literature includes an enormous amount of work that has been added to by generations of Buddha's disciples during the last two thousand and several hundred years, so it is difficult to discover the basic philosophy of Buddha from modern Buddhist studies. In contrast, if you read this book very carefully, I am sure you will find that what is written here is none other than the explanation of Buddhism taught by Buddha himself.

Buddha's Law is vast; like a great ocean, there is no end. Seawater tastes salty regardless of where you scoop it from; in the same way, although the Law I preach is boundless, it will always give you a taste of enlightenment no matter which part you choose to learn. Enlightenment as deep and wide as the ocean can nurture countless living creatures and give them ease.

Ryuho Okawa
Master & CEO of Happy Science Group
June 1993

PART TWO

Preface for Part Two

Part Two of this book continues to discuss the core concepts of Buddhist philosophies, such as the Middle Way, nirvana, emptiness, egolessness, and Buddha-nature, in a straightforward way. The publication of this new theoretical work on the spirit of Buddhism will significantly contribute to the deepening of the teachings of Happy Science.

The themes discussed in this book are rather technical, but I kept it one step short of an academic paper for the sake of many of my readers. Because this book mainly deals with metaphysical issues, I have tried to use colloquial expressions to make my explanations as easy as possible to read and understand, as I have done in my other books.

However, the main points I deal with are vital aspects of modern Buddhism and Buddhist studies. I assume that even those who have been studying Buddhism for a long time will feel that scales fall from their eyes and realize, "Wow, this is what Shakyamuni truly wanted to teach!" I hope that you will read this book very carefully.

Ryuho Okawa
Master & CEO of Happy Science Group
June 1993

CHAPTER ONE

Progress through the Middle Way

1

What Is the Middle Way?

The theme of this chapter is "Progress through the Middle Way." This is quite a tough theme. There are no writings that address *progress through the Middle Way* in any literature or doctrine related to Buddhism. And this is true not only in Buddhism but also in other philosophies. No one has ever directly addressed the theme, as far as I know.

Therefore, it is safe to say that progress through the Middle Way is one of the original themes of Happy Science. In other words, this is a very fresh theme and a theme befitting Happy Science.

I will start by giving the conclusion. What I mean by progress through the Middle Way is to aim for the improvement in human character and the prosperity of society through the right approach. That is to say, while exploring the right attitude to spiritual discipline in this life, endeavor to improve your character and work for the development and prosperity of society.

Perhaps you have come across the term *Middle Way* in other contexts. In politics, for example, people talk about a "middle-of-the-road" party. Here, "middle-of-the-road" is used to describe a party that is neither left- nor right-wing but in between. I wouldn't say this concept is wrong, but the Middle Way that Shakyamuni Buddha taught did not simply mean an idea or position located between two opposing concepts.

Similar to the Middle Way is the idea of the *mean*. The doctrine of the mean was part of Confucian thought, and Descartes, the origin of modern Western philosophy, taught this as *moderate*. I do not know precisely how Descartes understood it, but it seems he was advocating that when you encounter problems in life, it is better to find what is the most moderate and live in accordance with common sense when it comes to worldly matters. He probably thought that life was too short for you to become entangled in trifles that you did not know how to judge or handle. He thought that regarding trivial matters, it was better to follow common sense and the opinions of sensible people. Moderate, in his context, means something like, "a sensible way of thinking."

The question is whether mean and moderate are the same as the Buddhist concept of the Middle Way. There is a similarity, in the sense that they are balanced ways of thinking based on common sense, but in Buddha's teachings, the word "Middle" could be replaced by "Right."

The Middle Way means the right way. In other words, entering the Middle Way is almost synonymous with entering the Eightfold Path, which consists of Right View,

Right Thought, Right Speech, Right Action, Right Living, Right Effort, Right Will, and Right Meditation. I have given detailed explanations of the Eightfold Path in many of my writings, but the Path alone does not indicate what is right. In fact, what is right refers to "Middle" in the Middle Way.

Therefore, to understand the Middle Way means to understand what is right, and to understand what is right means nothing less than to understand the enlightenment that Shakyamuni Buddha attained. Let us think about the Middle Way from such a standpoint.

There are two main perspectives for discussing the Middle Way. One is to view the Middle Way as a practical approach—detailed principles for action, an attitude toward spiritual discipline, and a way of living. The other perspective is to view the Middle Way as a way of seeing or thinking or rather as a standard for making value judgments. In this chapter, I will discuss the Middle Way from both these angles.

2

The Middle Way as a Practical Approach—Avoiding Pain and Pleasure

First, I will talk about the Middle Way as a practical approach. Where did this philosophy of the Middle Way come from in the first place? It is an undeniable historical fact that Shakyamuni Buddha himself discovered the idea of the Middle Way in the process of attaining enlightenment.

Gautama Siddhartha was born in Kapilavastu, the royal palace of the Shakya clan, as the prince destined to be the future king. He was raised in luxury, with separate palaces for the summer, winter, and monsoon seasons, and he had a wife in each palace. He lived a life of material comfort until he was 29.

Although he lived very affluently, he became aware of the contradictions and impermanence of life, so he decided to set off in search of the answers to the questions that welled up within him. This was just after his wife Yashodhara gave birth to Rahula, his only son. He renounced the world and gave up everything, including his wives and son and his royal position. Although he sought a mentor who could give him answers to his questions about life, he could not acquire one. So he continued to practice ascetic training for six years, trying to seek enlightenment on his own.

During that period, he went through all sorts of physical discipline. For example, he cut down on all food until he was living on just a single grain and became skin and bones, or he meditated by burying his body in the soil—he underwent various ascetic training.

Even so, physical discipline could not provide him with the enlightenment he was seeking.

Note that Shakyamuni did not invent these practices of self-mortification. There are ascetics in India even now, but already in Shakyamuni's time, asceticism had been practiced for thousands of years. His ascetic training was based on yoga, a type of spiritual training with a history of several thousand years.

Shakyamuni's body became weaker and weaker, but just as his life was about to end, a young village girl named Sujata offered him a bowl of milk porridge. The moment he sipped it, he awakened to one truth: "I have been attempting to attain enlightenment by denying my life on this earth. However, terminating my earthly life does not in itself seem to lead to enlightenment. Because I have been given human life, it must be possible for me to find the true meaning and ultimate purpose of life by accepting it and making the most of it." With the goal of rebuilding his severely weakened body, he abandoned extreme asceticism and, as a result, entered the path to enlightenment.

In those days, there was a group of seekers undergoing ascetic training with Shakyamuni. On seeing him accept the milk porridge, they thought he had dropped out or given up on enlightenment. They despised him for this and left him.

Back then, the norm was that once you abandoned austere training, you became corrupt and were no longer on the path to enlightenment. In Jainism—a religion similar to and eventually became as large as Buddhism in India—it was believed that if you died while you were performing extremely harsh ascetic practices, you would become a saint. There was a clear line between Buddhism and the Jainist idea, which emphasized asceticism. In light of the traditional belief in austerity, Buddhism probably appeared to be a very easygoing religion.

However, Buddhism steadily developed and spread all over the world precisely because Shakyamuni abandoned asceticism and concentrated on the pursuit of enlightenment. In contrast, Jainism, which continued to emphasize ascetic discipline, has survived only in India and has not spread to other countries because its style was not universal.

So Shakyamuni reached the following conclusion: "Living at Kapilavastu until I was 29 years old, leading a life of luxury, rich in material comfort and pleasure, I was unable to find any of the answers to my questions about the true meaning of life. In a life of indulgence, I found only corruption, a path that led only to degeneracy, and a rejection of any possibility of improving human character. In such a life full of pleasure, affluence, and an abundance of food, I couldn't possibly have attained true enlightenment; it prevented me from refining my character. A life of extreme affluence and pleasure cannot lead people to true happiness, at least not to the happiness called enlightenment.

"On the other hand, the six years of asceticism tortured my physical body and would naturally have ended my earthly life. If the goal of spiritual discipline is to bring an end to one's life, then logically, this means we should never have been born on earth. Why were we born into this world to begin with? If ending one's life was the goal, there would be no meaning to one's birth. Ascetic training does not provide us with any of the answers to questions such as, 'Why did we come into this world?' or 'What is the purpose of life?' Rather, it encourages us to avoid answering these crucial questions."

That was Shakyamuni's conclusion. If the purpose of life was to simply deny the physical body, then it would be better not to be born into this world. Therefore, that does not answer the question about the purpose of life. In this way, he found that there was no improvement in human character by seeking pleasure, and with that being said, a life of pleasure was rejected. Furthermore, there were no ways to refine your wisdom and reason in the asceticism that needlessly tortures the physical body.

Even if you sit on a mat of thorns, stand on one leg for hours at a time, or stay underwater like a fish, it is most unlikely that your soul will be refined, that your awareness will be heightened, or that you will achieve progress supported by intellect or reason.

Buddhist philosophy started from Shakyamuni Buddha's endeavor to avoid both extremes and enter the Middle Way. This was the model that became the backbone of Buddhist philosophy. You must first know that. From a practical point of view, the Middle Way means rejecting the two extremes of pleasure-seeking and asceticism and entering the right way. What I mean by entering the Middle Way is not to live a mediocre life. Instead, it is a state of mind attained when you reject the extremes; you can only attain it after you clearly know that the extremes are not the answer. You will never attain this state of mind by living a mediocre or mundane life. Please remember that.

This is the Middle Way from a practical standpoint. I believe that this thinking should still be referred to today when seeking enlightenment.

Even today, many seekers practice austere training. Such practitioners are also in India and Japan. Some acquire the esoteric Buddhist title of Master by performing the Thousand-day Circumambulation in the mountains. There is no doubt that their physical strength is improved; perhaps they can develop mental strength as well. However, this training has nothing to do with enlightenment. Other kinds of Superman-like training have nothing to do with enlightenment, either.

On the other hand, of course, you cannot attain enlightenment by living a life of corruption—a life of indulgence and lust.

That is why it is important to be aware of the practical perspective that seekers can enter the path to enlightenment only when they discipline themselves and make an effort to refine themselves through the Middle Way.

3

The Point of View from the Middle Way

(i) Starting with a clean slate

Next, I would like to discuss the point of view from the Middle Way or how to interpret what you see. This is a more advanced interpretation of the Middle Way and is probably of greater importance to seekers.

What do I mean by the point of view from the Middle Way? Simply put, it means starting afresh with a clean slate. In Buddhism, it is sometimes expressed as *avyakata* (unanswered, unexplained). What it means is instead of blindly accepting conventional ideas and concepts and commonly accepted values, you should start from an unbiased viewpoint and see the world as it is.

Let me give you an example. In India, the caste system already existed at the time of Shakyamuni. The highest caste was the Brahmin or priest class. The second highest was Kshatriya, the warrior class. Below that was Vaisya, the merchant class. Then came Sudra, the slave class. There was even a class outside the caste system—Candala, the untouchables. People believed that the worth of a person was determined by birth. Shakyamuni asked straightforward

197

questions about the conventional caste system and spoke out against it.

Why were some people given the title Brahmin and respected since birth while others were labeled Sudra and considered ignoble? Did these castes really have anything to do with the true worth of a human being?

Shakyamuni's thoughts were revolutionary for his time. In short, he arrived at the following conclusion: "People are Brahmins by their deeds, Kshatriya by their deeds, Vaisya by their deeds, and Sudra by their deeds. Those who practice the way to serve buddhas and gods belong to the Brahmin class, those who work as warriors to the Kshatriya class, those who are involved in commerce to the Vaisya class, and the debauched who lead degenerate lives to the Sudra class. People's values are determined not by their birth but rather by their deeds. This is the right standard." That was his conclusion. By "deeds," he meant not only actions but also the will that gives rise to the actions.

This is what I meant when I said to think again, with a clean slate, about the values of human beings and their ways of living.

The society operates according to commonly accepted values, even today. One thing is judged to be of worth, whereas another is regarded as worthless. In areas such as work, gender, age, income, and appearance, people make worldly value judgments, but you should try to look at the world with a clean slate.

This is not to say skepticism is good. I am not telling you to doubt everything and destroy all value systems. What I mean is, instead of judging things on the basis of knowledge that has been handed down to you by others, you should look at everything in this world with a humble and open mind. Start from scratch, and take another look at things through your pure eyes. Then, you will find a completely different world unfolding before you.

Earlier, I used the example of the caste system. Now, let us take a look at educational background. In general, going to a highly respected school is considered valuable. However, if we take a look at the individuals who have graduated from top schools, in the best instances, the personalities and abilities of such people have been enhanced by their education, resulting in them making a contribution to the world; but in other cases, these people may have become much too proud of their educational achievements, indulging themselves and eventually causing others pain. So we can conclude that having a prestigious educational background is of neutral value; sometimes it works for good and sometimes for evil. If used properly, it is beneficial, but if misused, it can lead people in the wrong direction. The same thing can be said about property.

Perhaps the same applies to love for the opposite sex. Love itself is not evil. If love was classified as evil, then there would be no preservation of humankind. On the contrary, if the love between men and women is considered unconditionally good, then it would naturally lead people to live as they desire, such as indulging in lust and become corrupt.

Here is the point I would like to make. If you want to judge whether or not a particular way of life improves a person or takes them to true happiness, you need to look at the world with a clean slate. Look at worldly values with an unprejudiced eye, and find the right way of seeing from a spiritual perspective.

This is the first explanation of the Middle Way regarding the point of view. I believe people can easily understand this.

(ii) The Middle Way between continuity and discontinuity

However, the Middle Way does not end there. There is much greater depth to the Middle Way, an idea that has unfolded through history as a way of seeing, thinking, and making value judgments. Let us now consider this point.

In section two, I described the Middle Way from a practical standpoint: *the Middle Way between pain and pleasure*. It means neither pain nor pleasure is the answer. On the other hand, one way to understand the point of view from the Middle Way is *the Middle Way between continuity and discontinuity*. It can also be expressed as *the Middle Way of neither continuity nor discontinuity*. Here, let us consider the Middle Way between continuity and discontinuity.

This topic was much discussed in India during Shakyamuni's time.

Back then, people called the human ego *atman* and a divine being in heaven *brahman*. The mainstream idea was that both the self in each individual and brahman were of the same origin. It is true that the core of the human soul is formed of the same light as Buddha and that everyone has Buddha-nature within them, so this traditional idea of the Brahmins was not wrong; in terms of Buddha-nature, brahman (high spirits) and humans are one and the same. This idea is completely in line with what I teach today.

However, what would happen if it were to become a fixed idea? When you look around, you will find all sorts of evil being committed. Some people kill, some steal, some commit adultery, some live frivolously, and some invite bankruptcy into their families.

Observing such courses of life, you will find corrupt people, people who are failing, dejected people, or on the contrary, successful people. When humans ignore the differences between these two types of people and simply hold on to the idea that brahman and the self are one, they will neglect or dismiss the importance of their spiritual discipline and give up on it. This is their tendency.

Shakyamuni saw the danger in this simple idea that the self and the divine spirits are completely one, so he thought he must refute it. However, he was already aware that humans are spiritual beings who go back and forth between this three-dimensional world and the next, so he presented the idea of the Middle Way between continuity and discontinuity.

Continuity refers to the human ego or self that is perpetual. *Discontinuity* refers to the idea that human beings lose their ego upon death and that they become nothing after death. Such extreme views existed at the time. The former idea is a thinking of traditional Brahmanism based on the idea that humans have souls. The latter idea that everything terminates with death is a materialistic way of thinking that was also beginning to grow back then. The thought that everything ends with death is also strongly prevalent today. Shakyamuni shot back at those two ideas by advocating the idea of the Middle Way between continuity and discontinuity.

Shakyamuni meant: "Human beings do not disappear completely after death. In that sense, they are not discontinuous. However, what they think of themselves isn't continuous. This does not mean their body won't die; the being within their body won't be the same after they go on to the Spirit World."

What you consider yourself to be is based on the views that come from the six sensory organs—the eyes, the ears, the nose, the tongue, the tactile body, and the mind. Through these senses, you make various judgments and think that you exist. However, in the next life, the self based on these physical senses will not continue as it is.

The fact that there is life in the other world does not mean that what you consider to be yourself will go on to the other world in its current form. In the Spirit World, you won't have any sensory organs. Your body will take a more refined form called a spiritual body. For a short while after death, you continue to live as a spirit in human form, but as you become accustomed to life in the Spirit World, you will be able to live without taking on a human figure.

When you reach this state, you will understand that the form in which you now think yourself to be is not your true self. In the Spirit World, you can alter your form in any way you wish. You will continue to exist, but you will be different from your current self.

This leads to the conclusion that both the idea of continuity—the unchanging ego or self—and the idea of discontinuity—everything ends when you die—are wrong.

Thus, Shakyamuni taught, "Neither of them is true. You must enter the Middle Way." This is the idea of the Middle Way between continuity and discontinuity.

(iii) Misunderstanding the idea of egolessness

In later years, Shakyamuni's original intentions were misunderstood. As a result, his teachings of egolessness have been misinterpreted, as mentioned in Chapter Four of Part One.

Some people have gone so far as to assume that because Shakyamuni denied the ego or *atman*, there is no such thing as life after death.

If this view were right, it would mean Shakyamuni taught materialism. It would mean he taught that materials and this earthly world are everything. And this misunderstanding has been continuing to this day.

Such misinterpretation of egolessness that leads to the theory of no-soul is still prevalent today. Some Buddhist priests have adopted such views. Also, many professors of religion and Buddhist studies are teaching this wrong view on egolessness at universities. I have already taught you that the monks who do religious work based on such ideas head to hell after death. In the end, this is where they made their mistakes.

The correct answer is the following: "Your ego, namely yourself, is not a permanent existence. But the fact that you don't continue to exist does not mean that death is the end. Neither is it right to think that you are permanent nor is it right to think that you disappear at the time of death and are terminated. In reality, humans are beings that change and transform as they live."

Because people cannot understand this, when they are taught that "Humans are impermanent, and there is no ego. Egolessness is the truth about human beings," they misinterpret it as materialism; they think, "Souls will also disappear after death. There is no world after death."

When this sort of materialism spreads, it prevents people from living a spiritual life. These people tend to focus only on their earthly lives, and as a result, they pursue pleasure and surrender to the temptations of devils. This is a fundamental mistake.

Shakyamuni explained egolessness in the following way: "Human beings cannot live alone; they must live in harmony with others. If we all had sharp horns like a bull or a deer, we would hurt one another. If you have horns, you will get caught up in many things and suffer from them. Because you live in a society with other people, take care of your horns and trim them well. You should control yourself." That was the teaching of egolessness.

Egolessness could also be expressed as "not self." Shakyamuni also taught, "You do not exist alone in this world. You live only with the assistance of many other people. Because Buddha has allowed you to be, you exist. You cannot exist by yourself. When you realize that it is not you, yourself, who enables you to live, you are on the path to self-improvement and harmony with others."

However, people misunderstood Shakyamuni's teaching to eliminate the attachment that comes from a self-centered perspective; they took it as the denial of the physical self. I'm sure you all understand how it would be interpreted this way if you lack wisdom.

This misunderstanding of egolessness is one of the most critical mistakes in the history of Buddhism. It still continues to this day. There are many famous scholars who believe in this, too.

However, if you look at the idea of Shakyamuni, neither continuity nor discontinuity—the Middle Way between continuity and discontinuity—you can clearly tell that he was not supportive of the fact that death means the end and that he did not think in such a way. People have overlooked this part, too.

Irresponsible religious scholars and religious groups have, at times, attempted to criticize right religions using this mistaken view of egolessness. They say, "Because Buddha's teachings reject the existence of the soul, there are no spirits or the other world. Your religion is wrong." We must fight such an idea with firm resolve using the logic I have outlined.

If spiritual beings and the other world did not exist, then there would be no basis for the existence of religion itself. Ethics would be enough to teach people how to live in this world; there would be no need for religion. Religion is based on the fact that the other world, the world after death, or the world of spirits, exists. Religion exists to teach people how they should live in this world from the perspective of the other world. So don't be so foolish as to accept the views that deny the whole basis for the existence of religion.

When Happy Science believers try to convey the Truth to others, they will probably encounter the idea that humans have no souls, based on the false view of egolessness. At that time, they must firmly refute it. They may find themselves arguing with a priest, a religious leader, or a religious scholar, but they must resolutely break through such misunderstanding and ignorance of the fundamentals.

Human beings are inclined to adopt extreme views, such as "The human self continues forever" or "Death puts an end to everything." However, extreme views like these never convey the truth about life, so it is crucial that you see things through the Middle Way. The Middle Way with regard to the point of view means that you must start again with a clean slate and think truly and deeply about things.

(iv) The Middle Way between existence and non-existence—what is emptiness?

Another example of the Middle Way regarding the point of view, from the traditional way of thinking, is "the Middle Way between existence and non-existence." In other words, it is the Middle Way between the denial of existence and the denial of non-existence.

Ever since Shakyamuni's time, there has been a long-standing debate about whether human beings and material objects really exist. It is the human tendency to take simple and extreme views, such as things either exist or do not exist, and human beings either exist or do not exist. Shakyamuni kept his distance from both of these extreme views.

He thought, "What we see with the eyes seems to be real. No one can deny the fact that objects seem to exist—when you touch something, you feel it, and when you tap it, you hear a sound. Its existence cannot be denied. But the mere presence of something does not mean it is truly substantial or it truly exists.

"Then, can you say that what is not substantial does not really exist? Do desks not exist? Or do human beings not exist? You can't say they don't." This was the starting point of his teaching on existence and non-existence.

The debate on whether things really exist led to the idea of emptiness.

If we take into account the existence of the Spirit World, the concept of emptiness can be easily explained. Things in this world are not essential, substantial, unchangeable, eternal, or real. Only what exists in the Spirit World is real; the things of this world are temporary. Explained from a spiritual perspective, the concept of emptiness is very simple.

Nevertheless, people usually have difficulty understanding the spiritual world, so it is necessary to explain the idea of emptiness in worldly terms. The truth is that it is simple to explain that this world is temporary and the other world is real, but because many people have no understanding of the other world, they have difficulty grasping the concept of emptiness.

An explanation of emptiness that even worldly people can understand—such as those who don't know religion—is as follows:

Suppose I ask the question, "Does the Nagara River[4] really exist?"

Some people would say, "Yes. The Nagara River really exists." Then, I would ask them to bring it and show it to me. Which part is the Nagara River? Even if they brought me a bucket of water and told me, "This is the Nagara River," would that really be it? It might be some water from the river, but it would not be the Nagara River itself.

Similarly, let's say you brought some soil from the banks of the Nagara River. Could you claim that the soil was the Nagara River itself? Most likely, no.

Suppose someone took out a map and said, "The Nagara River starts here and ends where it meets the sea. This line of water is the Nagara River." Does this explanation really define the Nagara River? No, it doesn't.

Then, what is the Nagara River?

Imagine that you stopped the flow of the river. You dam the river upstream and downstream without leaking any water and bring all the soil and water as if you were displaying a miniature garden. Then, you say, "This is the Nagara River." Would that be an adequate explanation of the Nagara River? Is it possible to stop the flow of a river? Would it still be a river if it were dammed? Probably not. It would be a pond or a lake and no longer a river.

If so, the topic of the argument would change. "Although it is called Nagara River, does it really exist?" No one can pick up the actual Nagara River and explain what it really is. Nevertheless, we all call it the Nagara River and recognize that it exists.

In this way, things in this world have names and appear to exist, but you cannot point to or show their real substance—show something that is unchanging.

Think about the human body. Every day, old cells die and new cells are produced. Not one cell in your body is the cell you were originally born with. None of the cells are the cells you had 10 years ago. The same goes for your bones and even your brain cells. Every day, your brain cells are perishing.

Someone may ask you, "Who are you, really? Can you show me what you really are?" But even if you try, the moment you point to something, it will already have undergone changes.

In this world, there is nothing anyone can take out and say, "This is my unchanging self," "This is the human being who goes by my name," or "This is the Nagara River."

Everything is in a state of change. Everything is impermanent. This state of constant change or impermanence is explained by the term *emptiness*.

Just as you cannot clearly define the Nagara River or yourself by saying, "This is the Nagara River" or "This is me," you cannot prove that *you* of yesterday, *you* of today, and *you* of tomorrow are exactly the same being. Your body of yesterday and your body of today are different. Tomorrow, some parts of your body will have changed. As you eat different food, the cells of your body change accordingly.

Then, let's say you got rid of your body. Would it be true to say that your mind is your true self? Was your state of mind yesterday the same as your state of mind today or your state of mind tomorrow? What was in your mind yesterday is different from what is in your mind today, and what is there today is different from what will be there tomorrow. Even today, in another minute, your state of mind will be different from your state of mind now. Your mind will be different before and after you read this book. So even the mind cannot be your true nature—your real entity. You cannot take something that is fixed and say, "This is my mind."

The concept that everything is in a state of constant change is called *emptiness*.

However, I would like you to understand that so far, I have explained emptiness on the basis of this three-dimensional world so that the people in this world can understand it. Therefore, please be very careful; this explanation of emptiness could be misunderstood and taken for materialism. But for those who are not familiar with the Truth, you can probably use this explanation of emptiness as an expedient means.

Of course, the true meaning of emptiness is much deeper than this simple explanation. The real meaning of emptiness should be explained in terms of the relationship between this world and the other world or between the temporary world and the Real World.

So can we say that the Nagara River exists? It appears to exist, but we cannot assert that it really does exist. On the other hand, can we say that the Nagara River does not exist because we cannot take it out and show it? The water of the Nagara is flowing, so we cannot claim that the Nagara River does not exist.

The true nature of the Nagara River is to be found after denying simple assertions that the river exists or does not exist. The truth lies in the Middle Way, discovered after these extreme views have been rejected.

Seeing human beings and their surroundings, all the objects and phenomena on earth, from the perspective of the Middle Way between existence and non-existence—this was Shakyamuni's way of thinking. This is, in fact, the right way of thinking, as you can see from the explanations above.

According to the Buddhist view, what is right cannot be simply explained by saying, "If this is right, that cannot be right" or "Which is right, this or that?"

In Buddhism, what is right is explored in the following way: things that exist relative to other things are not real. For example, the relationship between you and me, or the relationship between this object and that object, is not substantial. This leads to the idea of emptiness.

When you deny the relative world, the world of the absolute emerges; this is one way to explain the spiritual worldview. To put it simply, a way of seeing things as existing individually or separately, such as you and I or this and that, is a relative view of the world. When you reject this view, the world of emptiness will open up before you, and in it, you will see the world of the absolute.

In conclusion, emptiness means to reject the idea that earthly existence is real. This shows people a way of thinking that allows them to get rid of earthly attachments. The concept of emptiness is a teaching to help people get rid of attachments to worldly things so that they can see what is truly valuable.

4

The Harmonious Union of the Threefold Truth

I would like to now go into the next explanation of the Middle Way.

The Chinese Buddhist philosopher T'ien-t'ai Chih-i (538–597 AD) thought of the concept of emptiness as follows: there are three perspectives or viewpoints of the Truth, which are the truth of emptiness, the truth of temporariness, and the truth of the middle. These are known as the Threefold Truth.

The truth of emptiness is a theme central to Buddhism, especially Mahayana Buddhism, which tries to free all people from worldly attachments and lead them to the Real World. The concept of emptiness is closely related to the idea of salvation advocated by Mahayana, or the Great Vehicle movement. This is the first important point.

"First comes denial—nothing in this world is substantial or real. Nothing earthly is truly substantial. There is no such thing as the physical body. Neither are clocks, desks, or all of you. They are all changing continually; they are all impermanent. Everything on this earth appears to be permanent, but it is only temporary and by no means substantial. It is not made by Buddha. It is not how Buddha intended it to be. What we see in this world is just a split second in the process of constant change, so if we want to understand the essence and true nature of all things, we must first abandon our earthly perspective. Only after this will the truth appear." This is the truth of emptiness.

However, what would become of the people who are content with the truth of emptiness? They would only be attracted to the Spirit World where Amitabha Buddha exists and neglect the earthly life. When Shakyamuni was practicing asceticism, there came a moment when he felt he should end his own life; he thought the path to enlightenment meant putting an end to his earthly life. Even now, there are seekers who think like this and believe that as long as they deny the physical body and the material world, they will attain the Truth.

The truth of emptiness is the first step to the Truth, but if you are satisfied with this level of understanding, there would be no meaning to your life and spiritual training on earth. So you must not stop here.

Next, you should also reject the truth of emptiness. That leads to the truth of temporariness.

"It is correct that the true nature of this world is emptiness and that all things and phenomena on earth are temporary, yet they actually exist for the time being. Because human beings undergo spiritual discipline in this world, we must accept the existence of this world and live in it. So it is not enough to simply deny everything. Yes, life on earth may be like a dream or an illusion, but it is an undeniable fact that there is an 'I' who is actually living here. If so, denying this fact will not in itself lead us to the attainment of the Truth.

"After first accepting the truth of emptiness, which is an idea that denied the existence of this earthly world, you must reject this truth itself and take into consideration the existence of earthly life, although it is only temporary." That is the truth of temporariness.

In philosophical terms, this idea is similar to existentialism. If you accept the existence of this world and think that it exists for your soul training, you need to find a positive meaning in earthly life and make an effort to develop as a human being here on earth. You should appreciate this world as the temporary truth.

However, if you are too attached to this idea, you will become comfortably settled in this earthly world and forget spiritual truths. If you feel that this world is easy and comfortable to live in and that it brings you happiness, you will have attachments to this world and will forget the other world.

In short, you first attained the state of the truth of emptiness, or the state of denying this world, and then attained the state of the truth of temporariness, but now you must reject this also.

What comes after that? It is the truth of the middle. A true way of living is found in being attached to neither the truth of emptiness nor the truth of temporariness but in the middle of those truths.

This is the explanation of the Threefold Truth that T'ien-t'ai Chih-i taught.

He believed that the Truth is to be found in the harmonious union of the Three Truths. He taught, "When you unite those three ways of thinking, you will discover the Truth."

The truth of the middle can be explained in the following way.

"You must know that the Spirit World exists. However, you must not neglect earthly life because the way you live in this world is closely connected to the way you will live in the Spirit World. This world is a training ground where human beings undergo spiritual discipline and refine their souls, so you must value your life on earth, but, at the same time, you must not forget the existence of the other world.

"In other words, when you think about the other world, you must never forget the perspective of this world, and when you think about your training on earth, you must never forget the perspective of the other world.

"It is likely that your mind will swing toward either the truth of emptiness or the truth of temporariness. However, you must not hold on to either of them but find the Middle Way between them. Combine the two truths, and there you will see the truth of the middle."

The truth of the middle describes T'ien-t'ai Chih-i's understanding of the Middle Way. He thought that while living in this world, we need to be aware of the truth of the world beyond this. While knowing the truth of the world beyond, it is necessary to find positive meaning in worldly life, but this must not lead to attachments to earthly living; rather, we must make further progress as a soul. Life of the Middle Way, which comes out of the harmonious union of the Threefold Truth, is the most desirable way of living based on the spiritual view of life.

Eventually, this philosophy goes back to the conclusion I outlined at the beginning of this chapter: Truth is not to be found in pleasure or in harsh austerity. The attempt to pursue truth through pleasure leads to a materialistic perspective, which leads people to mistakenly think of this world as reality. On the other hand, ascetic practices deny this world, and this idea would ultimately lead to the physical body and materials becoming entirely unnecessary. But the truth does not lie in either of them.

The Truth only lies in the Middle Way, and I explained that through the Threefold Truth: the truth of emptiness, the truth of temporariness, and the truth of the middle. You must think about the spiritual life and viewpoint without neglecting the way of life in this world that is backed by the viewpoint that spirits are real entities.

When you actually feel, "I am here, now," remember to always reflect on yourself from both the spiritual and the worldly perspective. If you always remember the spiritual perspective while making an effort to work toward development, self-improvement, and prosperity on earth, you are making progress through the Middle Way.

CHAPTER TWO

Hinayana and Mahayana

1

Criteria of Bodhisattva

The topic of this chapter is Hinayana and Mahayana, or Lesser Vehicle and Great Vehicle movements.

I introduced them for the first time in 1987 when I gave my first lecture, "The Principle of Happiness."[5] Now, I would like to explain Lesser Vehicle and Great Vehicle.

When Shakyamuni Buddha was alive, there was of course no distinction between the Lesser Vehicle and the Great Vehicle in his teachings; everyone in the order was disciplining themselves and doing missionary work under his guidance. In those times, both teachings were included, which later came to be known as the Lesser Vehicle and the Great Vehicle. But at that time, the main activity of the order was the spiritual discipline of renunciant disciples. As Buddha taught these mendicant seekers, the differences in their levels of ability gradually became apparent, and he acknowledged these differences.

There were two criteria for determining different levels of ability. One was the number of years a disciple spent studying the Law or the number of years that had passed since their ordination. The other was a disciple's level of enlightenment. Of course, this was a more appropriate criterion.

At Happy Science, we use the term *arhat*. Great importance is placed on whether a person has achieved the state of arhat. Those who have become an arhat are considered to have completed the first stage of spiritual discipline.

Who and when a person becomes an arhat has nothing to do with the length of time a person has been studying the Law; rather, it depends on their state of mind and how deeply they have studied. When someone seemed to have become an arhat, it was customary for a senior disciple to report it to Buddha, who then acknowledged it.

In short, the disciples of Shakyamuni's Sangha were evaluated by the number of years they had been disciplining themselves and whether they had achieved the level of arhat.

There were other spiritual levels besides arhat.

First was the level of *stream-enterer*, which was the lowest level. Those people firmly believed in Buddha's teachings and had entered the path to spiritual discipline.

The next level was *once-returner*. Those belonging to this stage were considered capable of reaching the level of arhat if they took on spiritual discipline in their next life. They may not be able to reach the state of arhat in this life, but because they are quite serious about disciplining themselves, they may be able to become arhats in their next life.

Above this was the level of *never-returner*. It refers to professional seekers who had reached a degree of spiritual discipline that was clearly higher than lay believers. It means that the 5, 10, or 20 years of spiritual discipline and the level of achievement they attained will help prevent them from easily falling back.

Simply put, any person who had reached this level had finished their mandatory reincarnation on the six paths of the Realm of Desire; in the next life, they would go on to a world of higher spirituality, the Realm of Form. In their next life, these never-returners would be born of their own will, with a clear aim and mission, rather than being reborn simply to satisfy their desires.

(According to Buddhist studies, the one who has reached the level of never-returner will not be born again, but this is not true. In India, during the days of Shakyamuni Buddha, there was an extreme view on reincarnation that said people were reborn into this world within 49 days after death, either as human beings or as animals. However, this is a mistaken view. What Buddha really meant was that those who had attained the spiritual level of never returner could lead a highly spiritual life in the world of high spirits, though they would eventually be reborn after several hundred years.)

The stage of never returner, however, does not imply a state of spiritual perfection; above this is the level of arhat. At this level, the person has finished studying the teachings and removed all the rust and dirt from their mind. They have a halo radiating from the back of their head. In most cases, their window of the mind has opened, so they can communicate with their guardian spirit. In short, they have finished eliminating their own delusions; this is considered to be the highest possible level one can attain as a seeker of the Truth. It is a matter of individual discipline up to this point. These are the levels you must go through in terms of individual study or self-reflection.

Above this is the stage of bodhisattvas. Naturally, all bodhisattvas are arhats. If they are not arhats, they cannot possibly be bodhisattvas. To become a bodhisattva, you must satisfy the conditions of an arhat and, at the same time, be able to skillfully teach and guide others. You need to have the ability to save others and actually practice it. Bodhisattvas are those who have built experience in saving others and have made achievements while maintaining the state of arhat.

Saving a drowning person in the river may usually be considered an act of bodhisattva, but a person cannot be classified as a so-called professional bodhisattva without having gone through proper spiritual discipline. A professional bodhisattva is someone who has studied the Truth well, has finished a certain level of individual spiritual discipline, and has been successful in saving people. That is the condition of a bodhisattva. Some people do not make an effort to perfect themselves but only go out to save others—

these people may believe they are saving others, but in many cases, they could be heading in the wrong direction.

This is the questionable part of those who teach faith in other-power. They say they will save others from misfortune, but oftentimes they could merely be earning money, like a business. They might really believe that they are saving other people, but in actual fact, those people are not being saved. Therefore, what they are doing is not a deed of a bodhisattva.

Suppose one of them said, "The water springing from this land is holy water, or virtuous water, so if you drink it, your illness will be cured and you will be saved." Then, they go around spreading it to many people. Although they may think that they are doing bodhisattva's work, if the water does not have any healing powers, then it is just a fraud. Many people think they can save others in this way without making an effort to discipline themselves, but this is quite a dangerous position to be in.

(In many new religions, people tell believers that if they bring others to the religion, they will instantly attain the state of bodhisattvas. But in many cases, what they consider bodhisattva is merely equivalent to the fifth-dimensional level, although the real bodhisattva level is of the seventh dimension. The reason for this is that in many of these new religions, the leader's level of enlightenment is not very high, and the level of followers is judged according to the leader's standard.)

2

Shakyamuni Buddha's Disciples

Shakyamuni Buddha taught, "First, work to develop a strong inner self. However, if you are concerned only with your own improvement, you may become egotistical, so remember to work toward teaching and saving others as well. Both types of effort are needed for you to perfect yourself as a seeker."

Buddha did not use the word *bodhisattva* in his lifetime. The word itself was introduced later on—people of the Mahayana movement mainly used this term. They used it to refer to those who were disciplining themselves to become a tathagata. But the idea of bodhisattva was already there in Shakyamuni's time.

In those days, his disciples disciplined themselves, studied the teachings, went around asking for alms, and conveyed the Truth. They visited people to give them guidance for life. So in this sense, the work of bodhisattva already existed in the time of Buddha.

When his disciples went out to pass on the teachings to others, Shakyamuni advised them to go not in twos but alone. If his disciples went in different directions, they would be able to meet and help more people. It was also training for them; by going alone, they would truly feel that their study of the Truth was insufficient. Through persevering in solitude, they would gradually become strong enough to conquer their anxiety or their lack of power to save people.

If they went to visit people in twos, things would be easier. It would be possible for them to play roles like actors before an audience and say they are great disciples of Buddha. For example, if one of them says, "He is a very great person. He is one of the 10 great disciples of Buddha," and the other nods, they can preach to the people as if putting on a show. But if they went alone, they wouldn't be able to put on an act; they would only be able to count on their own abilities. With those things considered, Shakyamuni often told his disciples: "Do not go with a companion. Go alone." This was the spirit of missionary work.

On the other hand, Jesus Christ dispatched his disciples in twos, but this was because the social background was different; in those times and in that region, it was dangerous to go out alone. In contrast, in Shakyamuni's time, his order had already won recognition in the area, so it was not very dangerous for his disciples to go out alone on missionary work. This is the influence of Buddhist philosophy that embraces peace.

(However, in Shakyamuni's later years, there was a rule that disciples could only go into town alone in the morning to collect alms. In the late afternoon or evening, they were strictly told to go out with a companion [according to the Nirvana Sutra].)

So in Shakyamuni's time, although self-discipline was essential, the work of salvation was also considered very important.

After Buddha passed away, a council was assembled to compile his teachings. In those days, however, there was no written language, so the disciples gathered in a cave and recited what they had learned and memorized. Ananda, who had attended to Buddha for 25 years, remembered the teachings very clearly, so the other disciples listened to him recite what he knew, and when they confirmed that what he had said was correct, they memorized it. Upali, who had a good memory for precepts and rules, recited each of them, and as each one was agreed upon, they memorized it.

In those days, the major part of the disciples' study was to memorize the teachings of Buddha. Also, they each practiced self-reflection and went out to preach to laypeople. Those were their main subjects of study.

Nowadays, however, Happy Science has books, CDs, and DVDs. Things are as modernized as ever. Generally speaking, disciples have little work now that such modern devices have been produced. Before they were invented, it was the disciples' job to memorize their master's lectures accurately and to talk about them to others; for example,

"In the first lecture, Master talked about such and such." But now that there are DVDs and other media, my disciples need to go further and explain my lectures, which is a higher level of work.

They need to not only be able to accurately talk about what they have learned but also study more deeply in order to give deeper explanations. This is the level required of them.

Buddha's teachings were memorized and handed down by word of mouth, even after his death. It was not until 200 or 300 years later that the teachings were written down in the form of sutras. The oldest sutras were written on the long leaves of tall trees called *tala*. These leaves had holes punched in them and were bound into book form with a string. But long before these sutras were compiled, all the teachings were passed down by word of mouth.

In India, in those days, people could memorize quite well because they had exceptional ability to memorize things. It appears they had such good memory that what they recited was more accurate than what was written down.

3

Hinayana Buddhism and
Mahayana Buddhism

As time passed, it seemed there was fear that Buddha's teachings would be lost unless something was done, so his disciples gathered several times to set down the teachings. First, they formulated a code of discipline in the form of the "250 precepts for monks" and the "348 precepts for nuns." They tried to strictly keep to this style of discipline to preserve the original teachings of Shakyamuni Buddha, or else they felt the teachings and disciplines might be distorted.

A few centuries after Buddha passed away, these disciples formed a fairly influential group, which in later years was called Hinayana Order. This group heavily focused on the precepts and formal procedures for discipline. Hinayana Order consisted only of renunciant disciples. While Buddha was alive, it was considered that only those who gave up their secular life would be able to attain enlightenment through spiritual discipline, and the Hinayana movement was formed to keep this tradition alive.

The sutras containing the traditional teachings of Shakyamuni Buddha remain to this day and are collectively known as the Agama Sutras. Agama Sutras is the generic name for Hinayana sutras. Therefore, the term *agama* has a very wide meaning—all sutras read and observed by Hinayana Buddhists are referred to as agama.

The Agama Sutras are mostly in Pali, one of the colloquial languages of ancient India, and the groups that adhere to these sutras are called Hinayana schools.

These teachings, known as Southern Buddhism, later spread southward to Sri Lanka and other countries of Southeast Asia. Even today, we find many Buddhist monks in Myanmar and Thailand who practice Hinayana Buddhism. They make much of observing the precepts, and in principle, they remain celibate. Strict adherence to traditional rules is characteristic of Hinayana schools. This is Southern Buddhism.

Meanwhile, later scriptures were written in Sanskrit, an ancient Indian language that was originally invented as a written language. In that sense, it is somewhat similar to Latin. Scriptures written in Sanskrit were compiled as Mahayana sutras. These teachings, known as Northern Buddhism, were conveyed to the northern part of India, Tibet, China, and Japan. Most of the Buddhist sutras that came to Japan are Northern Buddhism, also known as Mahayana Buddhism.

Mahayana Buddhism appeared about 200 to 300 years after Hinayana, sometime between the first century BC and the first century AD. Around this time, new scriptures were written by the followers of Mahayana groups. Hinayana practitioners were already active 200 to 300 years before them.

There have been similar changes in the history of Christianity. First, there were the teachings of Jesus, and the Catholic Church adhered to them. In the Middle Ages, the Reformation occurred, and those who believed in the new teachings were called Protestants. Even today, the teachings of these two movements are considered different, but from the perspective of the heavenly world, Jesus gives guidance to both of them. As time passed, new teachings were considered necessary for the people, so angels of light were sent down to earth to form new sects of Christianity.

The same could be said of Hinayana and Mahayana Buddhism. In the early days, Hinayana groups tried to strictly observe the teachings, as there were many people who had correctly received things and heard of how things were like in Buddha's time. But as time passed, people became concerned with just the formalities; consequently, the original spirit of Buddhism—for instance, the spirit of mercy—was lost. A reformation became necessary, as it was heading in a dangerous direction.

In other words, the Mahayana movement was a kind of new religion back then. A new sect of Buddhism was necessary as the old Buddhism could no longer save people. For this reason, Mahayana schools emerged one after another.

4

Mahayana:
The Movement to Save the Masses

What were the differences in teachings between Mahayana (Great Vehicle) and Hinayana (Lesser Vehicle)? A vehicle is something that transports people. In other words, the vehicles analogy was used to refer to the teachings. Obviously, Hinayana Buddhists never refer to themselves as Hinayana. Hinayana was a name given by the Mahayana Buddhists to demean the earlier ones and make themselves sound better. In short, the latter group referred to the earlier group as the Lesser Vehicle.

On the contrary, the earlier group called themselves *Theravada*, which simply means a group that strictly follows Buddha's teachings. So they were a group that was more on the conservative side. Those that branched off Theravada were known as *Mahasamghika*. They were less strict on the precepts and later developed into the Mahayana movement.

(Recently, another prominent theory about the origin of Mahayana Buddhism has been presented in Japan by Buddhist scholar Akira Hirakawa. It suggests that Mahayana was born from the worship of Buddhist stupas [traditional Buddhist tombs] by laypeople. However, although it is true that Mahayana Buddhists did worship Buddhist stupas, it is unconvincing to say Mahayana Buddhism originated in this way. The massive numbers of sutras were due to the work of professional, renunciant disciples, and as a spiritual leader, I strongly believe that a new type of teaching will not spread widely unless a powerful energy field is created by a devoted religious leader. A religious reformation will not occur naturally out of object worship.)

Believers of Mahayana looked down on and pitied the Hinayana believers, calling them the Lesser Vehicle. The reason was that Mahayana followers thought Hinayana Buddhists were busy saving themselves. The renunciant monks and nuns were clinging to the idea that only the renunciant disciples who had given up their secular lives could attain enlightenment or be saved from suffering. If that were true, there would be no hope of salvation for laypeople; the only thing they can do is to make offerings to the monks and nuns and be of service to them. But would that really be enough?

So a new, democratic movement in Buddhism started with the intention of saving as many people as possible. Mahayana Buddhism is a type of democratized religion. It meant that the focus shifted to laypeople. The Mahayana teachings spread widely by involving lay people. People who believed in those teachings thought, "It is not enough to think that renunciant seekers are the only ones who could be saved. You cannot call that 'salvation of all humankind.' The laypeople must also be saved."

In reality, the renunciant disciples were simply pursuing their own philosophy or logic, and their words no longer had sufficient power to save people. That was the background behind the development of Mahayana teachings. Furthermore, some of the renunciants were bound by the codes of discipline, which led them to formalism. So the new Buddhist movement was established out of necessity.

Hinayana Buddhism does not accept Mahayana Buddhism as the teachings of Shakyamuni Buddha. They say Mahayana is not true Buddhism. But this idea is mistaken because Mahayana was a new movement that was started under the guidance of Shakyamuni in the heavenly world to meet the needs of the times; it was a "great vehicle" for the salvation of the masses.

In a nutshell, Hinayana says you won't be saved unless you renounce secular life and undergo spiritual discipline, whereas Mahayana takes a very generous and magnanimous approach: "All people who board this greater vessel, be it 500 or 1,000 people, can be carried across to the other shore, to heaven. Get on board; then you can ride it to the other side."

How did Mahayana Buddhism turn out later on? Within Mahayana Buddhism is a sect that adheres to the Lotus Sutra.

The sect teaches that anyone who recites the Lotus Sutra will be saved. Believers also insisted that people would be saved if they merely kept the Lotus Sutra with them. To stress the significance of this sutra, they even went to the extreme of saying, "You will not necessarily fall to hell if you speak ill of Buddha, but if you speak ill of the Lotus Sutra, you will fall to hell." The same holds true for Pure Land schools of Buddhism, which advocate that people would be saved in the afterlife if they recite the Three Pure Land Sutras— Buddha of Infinite Life Sutra, the Meditation on Buddha of Infinite Life Sutra, and the Amitabha Sutra. Simply chanting the name, Amitabha could also save them. The Pure Land schools are also part of Mahayana Buddhism, so it could be said that the Great Vehicle movement is a popularized form of religion.

However, there are two sides to everything. Hinayana observed Buddha's teachings quite strictly, so the original teachings remained intact; however, because Mahayana had been popularized, its missionary work gradually turned into a sort of business. It sought to gain as many believers as possible and took extreme measures.

For example, some Mahayana sects first said, "You will be saved just by reciting *Namu-Amida-Butsu* (I put my faith in Amitabha Buddha)," but gradually, the idea developed further: "The great Amitabha knows everything about you even before you chant *Amitabha*." Then it became "You will be saved the moment you wish for salvation" and "You will be saved without even wishing for salvation or even if you have done wrong." In this way, the idea developed even further to gain more believers.

I can understand the spirit behind this idea, but it is doubtful whether it has actually saved people in the truest sense. It has not really been investigated whether people were actually saved. So Mahayana Buddhism went to the extreme and spread far and wide, but at the same time, it degenerated and became corrupt.

Besides Mahayana and Hinayana, there is another branch called Esoteric Buddhism. To be precise, it should not be included in Mahayana Buddhism. Mahayana began mainly between the first century BC and the first century AD, but Esoteric Buddhism began much later—in India, sometime around the seventh century AD.

Esoteric Buddhism, although it calls itself a branch of Buddhism, has much more in common with Hinduism, which is an ancient Indian religion, and is mainly concerned with the pursuit of earthly profits and psychic powers. So the esoteric teachings transmitted from India to China are, strictly speaking, different from the Buddhism taught by Shakyamuni Buddha. Buddhism transformed itself to merge with a traditional Indian religion to survive—that is Esoteric Buddhism.

If something like that were to happen in Japan, it would be like Buddhism integrating with Shintoism and then practicing Shugen-do (ascetic training in the mountains).

However, around the time when Esoteric Buddhism was flourishing in China and when it was handed down to the Japanese monk Kukai (AD 774-835), it became something to be highly valued.

The original esoteric teachings of India, on the other hand, became corrupted later on and led Buddhism to decline. Followers of these esoteric teachings advocated the complete opposite of Buddha's teachings (sexual desire, for example, was positively affirmed) and spoke and acted in a radical way. In the end, they headed toward degeneration and finally disappeared.

5

Seeking Enlightenment Above and Saving People Below

I have spoken on the general picture of Mahayana and Hinayana. If I were to summarize the spirit flowing within them, it would be as follows:

In Buddhism, there is a commonly used phrase, *Seek enlightenment above and save people below*. In brief, this means you are supposed to seek as high a level of enlightenment as possible while trying to teach and save as many people as possible. This is indeed the fundamental spirit of Buddhism.

Seeking enlightenment above is the central theme of Hinayana Buddhism. As you pursue higher enlightenment, you are apt to avoid interacting with society, and consequently, you will need to renounce secular life and devote yourself to spiritual discipline.

On the other hand, if saving people below is your main concern, you are apt to disregard the precepts. Instead, you must save as many people as possible or awaken them to faith by working together with fellow believers. If this is the case, although Shakyamuni Buddha taught 84,000 teachings, you may want to ignore them and focus on leading people to faith simply by saying, "Just chanting *Amitabha* is enough" or "Just having the Lotus Sutra with you is enough." That is how far it can go if you take the idea of saving people to the extreme.

In the past, Buddhism experienced both of these extremes, and now it has lost its spirit.

Going back to the original purpose of Buddhism, it is very clear what we must do: we must aim to attain enlightenment and save people at the same time.

Humans tend to take the easy way and are apt to go in either direction because it is easier for them to follow a consistent path.

If they are taught that seeking enlightenment is important, then they may want to completely cut off from society and live in the mountains to discipline themselves in solitude. It may be easier for them to concentrate on their training, but it means that they have relinquished their responsibility to the world. Some ascetics live in the mountains alone for 12 years. They don't watch the news or read newspapers and have no clue what went on in society during those 12 years. They simply seclude themselves in a small temple to undergo spiritual discipline. Although this way of life should not be wholly condemned, these people do not seem to have the ability to save others.

On the other hand, although it is alright to work to save others, we find many Buddhist priests becoming secular and doing business to gain earthly profit. These degenerate priests have given up studying Buddhist teachings and disciplining themselves. Please be careful not to become like them.

What we have to do now is to try our best to integrate these two seemingly contradictory directions. We must not be discouraged by the contradictions, and we must not give up integrating these two goals.

That is to say, we have to be a group of people who seek enlightenment to no end and, at the same time, wish to save as many people as possible. This was taught in the original Buddhism. You cannot just choose one or the other.

Then, what should you do? As a seeker of Truth, you must first be strict with yourself in your attitude toward spiritual discipline and seeking enlightenment. But because you are to save others at the same time, you have to be kind toward other people. The attitude of seeking enlightenment above and saving people below means being strict with yourself while being kind and tolerant to others.

People generally tend to be either easy on themselves and easy on others or strict with themselves and strict with others. Those who tend to be easy on themselves are usually easy on others, saying, "You don't have to do so much." This is the usual case. Someone who cannot get good grades in school would want to tell others, "You don't have to work so hard. If you are pure in heart, that's enough." Indeed, people who are easy on themselves will be easy on others.

On the other hand, people who are strict with themselves tend to be strict with others too, saying, "Nothing else matters. You have to get full marks." This is extreme, too. So what you must do is seek both ways without going to the extreme.

Therefore, as a basic attitude, you have to be strict in disciplining yourself. You must never be easy on yourself. However, you must have a heart of kindness and mercy for others as much as possible. Kindness and mercy do not mean simply being easy on others. You must nurture others, so you need to use wisdom when you give love to them.

Hinayana and Mahayana still remain today as two different streams of Buddhism, but they must be brought back to the original spirit of Buddhism—"We are a group of people who seek enlightenment and, at the same time, a group of loving people who work to help and save others." We just have to put effort into integrating these two directions, and it solely depends on our mindset regarding spiritual discipline. It all depends on our mindset and attitude. Once you become easy on yourself, that will be the end.

CHAPTER THREE

What Is Nirvana?

1

Nirvana and Emancipation

In this chapter, I would like to talk about *the perfect tranquility of nirvana*, which is one of the Three Dharma Seals.

The first seal is *the impermanence of all things* or the idea that all things in this world are transient and impermanent and that nothing remains the same. With this idea, Buddha taught people to let go of their attachment to the things of this world.

The second seal, *the egolessness of all phenomena*, essentially conveys the same idea as the teaching of emptiness, the idea that all things in this world are non-substantial and that only the spiritual is real.

In short, the impermanence of all things and the egolessness of all phenomena are both teaching you not to be attached.

The "seals" in the Three Dharma Seals simply mean markers of the teachings. These three teachings are clear markers of Buddhism. All three of them focus on the importance of eliminating attachment, which signifies that this idea is central to the teachings of Buddhism.

The third seal is the perfect tranquility of nirvana, which is the main topic of this chapter.

First, let me explain the word *nirvana*. Nirvana (in Sanskrit) or *nibbana* (in Pali) is the word for the ultimate objective of Buddhism. It is the goal and purpose of Buddhist teachings.

The word can also be replaced by *emancipation*. These two terms are sometimes used interchangeably.

But strictly speaking, they are slightly different. Some say that these two words can be distinguished as follows: "The result of achieving emancipation is a state of mind called nirvana, so emancipation should be regarded as an active process through which one reaches the state of nirvana." They are almost synonyms, but some people point out the slight difference in meaning.

Then, what is emancipation? It means to become free from the bondage of this world, from all physical limitations. In other words, emancipation means to attain spiritual freedom, and the result of this is the state of mind known as nirvana.

2

Buddha's Fire Sermon

The word *nirvana* originally meant "to extinguish" or "to be extinguished."

So what is being extinguished? You are extinguishing delusion or the flame of worldly delusion.

What exactly is the flame of worldly delusion? Typical examples are the Three Poisons of the Mind: greed, anger, and foolishness.

Worldly delusion is a general term for the negative workings of the mind. There are numerous delusions; according to Buddhist tradition, there are 108 worldly delusions. These include all sorts of negative vibrations, ideas, and ways of thinking as well as actions based on such things; in general, they are called worldly delusions.

The representatives of those delusions are the Three Poisons of the Mind. They are greed, anger, and foolishness, also known as the three flames.

What does the word *flame* symbolize?

There is a very famous sermon given by Buddha, called the Fire Sermon, which is often compared to Christ's Sermon on the Mount.

In those days, in India, there was a fire-worshiping religion led by a man named Uruvilva Kasyapa. He was the eldest of three brothers, and they had a following of as many as 1,000. Buddha, who at that time only had several dozen followers, went to see the brothers and subdued them; he converted the fire worshipers to Buddhism. As a result, Buddha's order suddenly expanded to a group of over 1,000 followers. This incident made the order quite famous.

Buddha gave the following sermon before the fire worshipers:

The entire world is burning.
Look at the world. Everything is burning.
All things are burning.
What makes them burn?
It is the flame of worldly delusion
That arises from the human mind.
Fire symbolizes the blazing earthly delusions.

Therefore, do not worship fire.
Although you have been devoted to fire worship,
Fire itself is not holy.
It simply represents how worldly delusions burn within you.
So you must not take fire as something sacred.
Instead, extinguish it. That is important.

The entire world is burning
Because of the worldly delusions within you, human beings.

They are the cause of suffering in this world.
Only when the fire has been extinguished
Will you truly experience a tranquil, pure,
And serene mind.
This state of mind is what you, devoted seekers,
Should aim to attain.

So I say unto you,
You were practicing the wrong teachings.
From this point on, follow my teachings
And devote yourself to the right spiritual discipline.

This was the content of his sermon. I believe this is what it means to "extinguish."

In other words, human beings have greed; they are full of desires without having the mind that says, "It's enough." Also, humans have anger; they lose their temper when things don't accord with them and when they cannot have what they want. And there is foolishness; the act of complaining goes back to being a fool. Your own foolishness is expressed as words.

Greedy minds, angry minds, and foolish minds are the biggest causes of people's suffering.

3

The State of
the Perfect Tranquility of Nirvana

Nirvana is attained when all the delusions that derive from the physical body have been extinguished. This state of mind is exactly the same as that of an arhat. As the seeker of Truth, reaching the state of an arhat is the same as attaining the state of nirvana.

Nirvana can be described using the following metaphor.

In the mountains, there is a beautiful, quiet lake. There is no one around, and it is so calm that not a sound can be heard. The water is so clear that you can see the bottom of the lake. You get into a small boat, and as you look down to the bottom of the lake, you see many white shells and little pebbles.

These shells or pebbles signify the suffering we experience in this world. While living in this physical world, people experience various kinds of suffering, and many of them are struggling in the midst of such suffering.

However, someone who has achieved the state of nirvana can calmly observe the suffering he or she is going through— the pebbles or shells lying at the bottom of the lake—as if seeing through the clear water. This state is the perfect tranquility of nirvana.

If you achieve this state of mind while you are alive, you will no longer struggle with suffering but will instead see your problems quite objectively and calmly. You will think to yourself, "So this is the cause of my suffering. This was caused by a delusion that derived from the physical body. I have to let go of this right now. From a spiritual viewpoint, this is how my suffering appears." In short, you can see your state in this world and the cause of your suffering from the vantage point of the Real World.

Therefore, although humans face various kinds of suffering and worries during the course of their lives, those who have achieved the state of nirvana can look at their own problems and suffering as if they are looking down upon them from the Real World. And they aren't caught up by them; rather, they can pick out the problems and view them. Once you become an arhat, you will reach this state of mind.

4

Two Different Types of Nirvana

The state of nirvana, also called the realm of nirvana, can be classified into two types. One is called *nirvana with remainder* (also called *nirvana in the Dharma of the present*), whereas the other is called *nirvana without remainder*. The first type of nirvana is experienced when there is something on which it depends. And the second type of nirvana is when there is nothing on which it depends.

Now, what do they depend or not depend on? It is a matter of whether or not they depend on the physical body—in other words, the physical form. This is the main point.

Nirvana *with* remainder is the type of nirvana experienced while one still has human attributes, such as a physical body and worldly thoughts and feelings, or other impurities pertaining to a physical body. Nirvana *without* remainder can be attained when one dies, after one is rid of all earthly impurities.

Nirvana with remainder might also be called *emancipation during life*. It means that one has achieved the state of arhat while they are still alive in this world. Nirvana without remainder could therefore be called *emancipation without a physical body*.

We sometimes hear people say that a person has entered nirvana when they mean he or she died, but death cannot be the goal of life. The basis of Buddhism is for people to be able to enter the state of nirvana while they are still alive. This is the reason we practice spiritual discipline. The concept of nirvana aimed to teach people that they could attain the same peaceful state of mind in this world as in the world after death. That is what is meant by entering nirvana while being alive.

There is also the word *parinirvana* (*parinibbana* in Pali), which literally means perfect extinction or perfect nirvana. There is a Buddhist sutra called the Mahaparinirvana Sutra; *maha* means "great," and parinirvana means the death of a person who has achieved emancipation while alive. This is not a word used for ordinary people; it is only for those who have achieved emancipation in this world and who will then enter the final state of nirvana after leaving behind the physical body.

For example, when Mahatma Gandhi died, some people said he had passed into parinirvana. It refers to the death of such well-respected people or people who have attained a high level of enlightenment.

5

Non-Abiding Nirvana

There is yet another kind of nirvana, *non-abiding nirvana*.

The nirvana I mentioned earlier, or the two different types of nirvana—nirvana *with* remainder and nirvana *without* remainder—are concepts that have much to do with attaining enlightenment, so they are mainly used in Hinayana Buddhism.

Hinayana is a doctrine and a form of spiritual discipline among the renunciant disciples. It mainly focuses on the renunciant disciples and does not give much consideration to lay followers. In contrast, Mahayana is Buddhism intended for lay followers. The aim of the Mahayana movement was to spread the teachings of Buddha to lay followers. They thought that Buddha's teachings should not be limited to the renunciant disciples only but should be available to everyone. Mahayana focused on the lay followers and had a very wide perspective of salvation, but because of that the disciplinary aspect became weaker, just as I mentioned in the previous chapter.

Non-abiding nirvana is a new way of understanding nirvana that appeared in the Mahayana stream.

From the outset, nirvana was an idea central to Buddhism and, in a sense, the core of Hinayana Buddhism. Those who follow Hinayana aim to attain the state of arhat; that is their goal. So if such an idea is carried out as it is, Mahayana Buddhism will lose its argument and become groundless. If all Buddhist followers had devoted themselves to pursuing only their own emancipation and becoming free from the restraints of earthly life, then there would not have been a movement to spread the teachings to laypeople.

In fourth- or fifth-century India, two brothers named Asanga and Vasubandhu—who are like the revivers of Mahayana Buddhism—and other prominent monks thought it necessary to reinterpret the idea of nirvana to encourage the further development of the Mahayana movement. They proposed a new form of nirvana called non-abiding nirvana.

As you can see, it means a nirvana without abode—simply put, it is a nirvana where people would neither remain in the world of birth and death nor remain in the state of nirvana.

In Buddhism, *birth and death* generally refers to the repeated birth or cycle of reincarnation in the Realm of Desire. The world whereby people are bound by the chain of reincarnation is also called the world of delusion. These monks of the Mahayana movement began to assert that there should be another kind of nirvana in which people remain neither in delusion nor in the world of enlightenment—the pure and calm state of nirvana as taught by the Hinayana schools.

This is the state of bodhisattva advocated in Mahayana, and it is a proactive and dynamic idea of nirvana. This idea was developed as a criticism of Hinayana. Mahayana Buddhists thought, "We cannot be sitting in meditation and immersed in self-satisfaction and call it nirvana like Hinayana. Even after returning to the other world, we will not stay still in a high-dimensional spiritual world that has nothing to do with this world. Our main focus is on saving people.

"Our aim is to save people, so we must constantly be thinking about saving others with great mercy. It is out of the question to think that we will emancipate ourselves and stay put in nirvana while we are still alive. Neither can we accept that upon entering the high-dimensional spiritual world after death, we do not think about saving people."

They argued that even someone who could be a bodhisattva or a tathagata would dare to go to the world of delusions such as hell, the Astral Realm of the fourth dimension, or the Goodness Realm of the fifth dimension to help others. They would also be happy to be born again into this world to save those who are living on earth. Despite having attained the state of nirvana, they do not abide there but surpass birth and death, and nirvana. They strive solely to save people. With mercy, they would work tirelessly to save others. They called this state of mind non-abiding nirvana.

My comment on this, however, is that it is rather difficult to acknowledge this particular perspective of nirvana because the condition of nirvana itself would not make any sense. Let me explain.

The pure state of mind of nirvana is something that can only be attained by those who have actually experienced the suffering of the flame of worldly delusions and physical desires and have tried to extinguish it. It is only after they have successfully overcome such suffering that they are able to see others struggling in the flame of worldly delusion and advise them to extinguish it. Therefore, without the experience of achieving the state of nirvana, one wouldn't be able to tell that others are suffering in the flame of worldly delusion.

In general, religious groups say that their objective is the salvation of people, but unless the abovementioned point is understood, the followers of these groups will be trying to save others while they themselves are the ones who actually need saving. This is quite common. I see many religious groups that fall into this category.

Although the ideals of the Mahayana movement are commendable, there is always the question of whether those who are trying to help others have the qualities to do so. Unless these people have had the experience of attaining the true state of nirvana or the state of freedom from worldly delusions, they won't actually be able to help others.

Non-abiding nirvana is a unique and wonderful idea, but if it is taken to be an easy road to nirvana, it could lead to the danger of giving up the pursuit of enlightenment and instead focusing purely on commercial-like activities. In reality, the suffering owing to worldly delusion is quite difficult to understand unless you have had the experience of overcoming it.

Thus, although this Mahayana view of nirvana is noteworthy, it is rather hard to accept. After all, what we must do is seek the state of nirvana through emancipation from worldly delusions while simultaneously teaching and leading others based on our own experience gained on the way to enlightenment. This is the right attitude for a true seeker of Buddhism.

6

The Level of Enlightenment and the Power to Save People

What I just explained corresponds to the Happy Science teaching of *Benefiting yourself benefits others*. This means that you should first try to achieve true happiness by seeking a higher level of enlightenment so that you can also discover ways to teach and guide others to lead them to true happiness. Pursuing either one is not enough.

Buddhism often teaches you to benefit yourself, but this alone is not good; neither is it enough to act only to benefit others. In fact, only when you are able to both spiritually train yourself and help others in this lifetime can you be a complete human being. I would like you to aim to accomplish both.

A person's level of enlightenment is firmly connected to their power to save others. As you achieve higher levels of enlightenment—for instance, the bodhisattva or tathagata level—you will be able to teach and help more and more people. In fact, higher levels of enlightenment signify a greater ability to lead others to true happiness. Even if those at the fourth- or fifth-dimensional level were to strive to convey the teachings of the Truth, only a few people would actually be freed from suffering. That is why you must not forget this standpoint: the height of enlightenment leads to the power of saving.

The two different views of the Lesser Vehicle and the Great Vehicle are usually considered incompatible by most religious groups. People tend to be inclined in either one direction or the other, often failing to reach either goal, but you need to pursue both. In trying to overcome the contradiction, you will find the Middle Way.

If a group of people seeks enlightenment for themselves only, the idea of benefiting the self will be apt to become egoistic. One hundred years after Shakyamuni's death, Hinayana Buddhists became only focused on saving themselves. The renunciant disciples of Hinayana were all bound by the precepts, seeking only their own happiness and neglecting the lay followers.

Then, some disciples realized, "That's not the way it should be," and fundamentally split off from Theravada in the history of Buddhism. The majority of the people who were more tolerant of precepts gathered to form the Mahasamghika school. Such a school with free spirit experienced its early days—where it was further divided into multiple Buddhist schools—and then started the Mahayana movement. So both ideas are necessary—pursuing enlightenment and saving others.

To conclude, the Three Dharma Seals are a set of ideas given to teach people to abandon attachment to the things of this world.

"If you are living a life attached to the worldly delusions that mainly derive from the physical body, then you can neither attain enlightenment nor attain true happiness. So do not become attached to what is transient. That is what is meant by the impermanence of all things.

"Do not become attached to what is visible or tangible. That is the egolessness of all phenomena.

"Do not remain engulfed in the flame of the worldly delusions that mainly derive from your physical body. Extinguish the flame, and you will attain the state of true happiness. That is the teaching of the perfect tranquility of nirvana."

In this way, all three seals are teachings of abandoning attachment; they advise you to enter the Real World while you are alive. This idea is basic and central to the teachings of Buddhism. By now, you should have a fairly good understanding of the Three Dharma Seals of Buddhism.

(In addition to the three types of nirvana explained in this chapter—nirvana with remainder, nirvana without remainder, and non-abiding nirvana—there is yet another type of nirvana called *natural nirvana*. These are called the Four Kinds of Nirvana. The last type of nirvana is experienced when you see the pure heart shining like a diamond within you and understand that it is your true nature.)

CHAPTER FOUR

Emptiness and Salvation

1

The Idea of Emptiness and the Perspective of Causality

Although I have already explained the idea of emptiness in Part One, Chapter Five, "Emptiness and Causality," that discussion was not of sufficient depth to give you a deep understanding of such a significant concept, so I would like to discuss it again from another angle.

The idea of emptiness (*sunyata* in Sanskrit) is generally considered a key concept in Mahayana Buddhism, but this idea certainly did not develop when Mahayana appeared. Of course, it already existed during the time of Shakyamuni Buddha centuries ago.

Here, let me talk further about the meaning and significance of the word *emptiness*. "What is emptiness?" Sometimes people may answer, "Emptiness is causality." In some of the Buddhist scriptures, we find the following phrases: "The Dharma is causality. Those who see causality see the Dharma; those who see the Dharma see causality." If the Dharma were causality and emptiness were causality, then it might be true to say that the Dharma is both emptiness and causality.

Of course, they might not overlap each other 100 percent, but from this you can see how important the idea of emptiness is.

The essence of Buddha's teachings is the perspective of causality, and the significance of causality can be understood through exploring the idea of emptiness. I think you can comprehend it this way. Here lies one of the core concepts of Buddhism.

Shakyamuni Buddha gave many other teachings such as the Four Noble Truths and the Eightfold Path, of course, but when you delve further into them, you will find that they narrow down to the ideas of causality and emptiness, which are considered to be the core of all teachings.

Then, what does the phrase "emptiness is causality" mean?

Here, let us reorganize our thoughts on causality. The term *causality* means dependent arising, which is made up of cause, condition, and occurrence. It represents a way of seeing things in light of the chain of cause and effect.

Therefore, causality is an idea that has much to do with the passage of time. An example of this is the 12-fold chain of causality, which develops as follows: "Because of ignorance, there arises action; because of action, there arises consciousness; because of consciousness, there arises name-and-form (...)" (see Part One, Chapter Six). Obviously, this explains causality in the context of the passage of time, and it could be said that the formula of the 12-fold chain is a typical example of this basic type of causality.

Let us call this type *time causality*. There is another aspect of causality, which could be called *space causality*. (Note that these two terms are not traditional Buddhist terminologies; they are the terms I have coined.)

2

Space Causality

What is space causality?

It boils down to the idea, "the essence of all things is spiritual."

In other words, all things in this world appear to actually exist, but in fact they are not real; only the spiritual existences are real, and all else is just an illusion. Such a view of the world is the idea of space causality.

Although this may be a little materialistic, to enlighten people about such spirituality, various means are used to explain that all kinds of worldly things, human beings, and creatures do not have real substance in them.

For example, consider the following way of thinking:

If we break down all things to the level of molecules and atoms, then we would see nothing—blackboard, table, microphone, or whatever it may be. Tables, blackboards, and things that have their own name would not exist. The same goes for humans, too. Suppose there is an average-sized adult; if this person were to be reduced to the level of molecules and atoms, as if examined under a microscope, there would be no human being to begin with.

We refer to ourselves as *I* or *me*, but does such an independent being actually exist? You might call "this thing" an individual item or substance, but does it actually exist?

What is it that supports the being called *I* or *me*? If we consider these factors in depth, we will find that we are not only physical beings composed of molecules or atoms but also beings supported by many other factors, such as the food we eat three times a day. Because we eat, we are able to exist.

But where does the food we eat come from? Where does the bread we eat for breakfast come from? Where does the wheat used to make the bread come from? Perhaps from Australia or Canada.

Who produced the wheat? It was the foreign farmers who are complete strangers to us. In those countries is the land that experienced rainfall and where fertilizers were added so that the wheat would grow. The farmers worked to harvest it, perhaps using a combine harvester. Moreover, there were grain merchants and workers who loaded the wheat onto the freighters, which were constructed by shipbuilders. The wheat was then shipped to our country.

After it was imported, it was processed and made into flour; then, bread was made from flour. The bread was brought and distributed to the retailers, where consumers bought it. When you eat bread, perhaps you spread jam on it and have a glass of milk with it. Where does the milk come from? Cows of which dairy farm?

So our everyday life is actually connected to every part of the world. *I* or *me* is closely connected to the lives of many different people living in many countries all over the world. If this is the case, not only our individual will but also the activities of all living beings and the workings of everything that exists on this globe allow us to exist as we are.

Of course, there is also the governing of the country. There is a country called Japan; it has its society, organizations, and people who work there, and they receive their pay. They are all allowing you, a person, to exist.

What it means is that you are blessed by every single thing that exists on earth—both living and non-living things—and with their blessings, you are able to live a day.

3

Emptiness and the Three Dharma Seals

As I explained, not only in terms of time causality but also in terms of space causality, the fact that something exists in this space now is because of the accumulation of numerous workings and substances that we do not see. What appears to exist here at this time certainly does not exist on its own.

Take a single human body, for example. It exists thanks to things like bread or rice. If those supplies were to stop, the physical body itself would deteriorate. Also, bread or rice is produced not only by the work and effort of many people but also thanks to the blessings of nature, such as sunshine and rain. We are alive thanks to the existence of all things on this earth, including the heat and energy of the sun.

If you look at things in such a way, you will really understand the teaching of egolessness. "Nothing in this world exists on its own. Nothing in this world truly exists in its original sense. Everything is made thanks to various things supporting each other."

The *kanji* character for "human"(人) is in the shape of two sticks supporting each other. It is also sometimes said that it takes after the shape of rice bundles leaning against each other after harvest.

Just like that, people exist because of the support they give to each other. If people can only exist because of each other's support, we can say that their existence is based on emptiness. They currently appear to exist owing to the support of many other elements.

In this case, emptiness means almost the same as space causality. But because it takes time for the grains to grow until they are ready to be harvested and finally made into bread, emptiness may also include the aspect of time causality.

So there are two elements to this idea: causality in relation to time and causality in relation to space.

To put it another way, time causality corresponds to the idea of the impermanence of all things, which means that all things are transient and nothing remains the same in this world. In short, "the impermanence of all things" means everything is changing. If you become attached to things that are transient, you will only suffer. So when you become deeply aware that all things are transient and will disappear someday, you can let go of attachment. Time causality can therefore be an explanation of "the impermanence of all things."

Space causality, on the other hand, could be close to "the egolessness of all phenomena."

The third seal of the Dharma is "the perfect tranquility of nirvana," which signifies the state of mind of someone who has eliminated all attachment and is emancipated from all bondage of this world. But this does not mean they are in the state of nihilism and that all things vanish.

When you have abandoned your attachments and become emancipated, what world would appear there? What is the state of the perfect tranquility of nirvana? Does it mean there is nothing at all?

No, it does not mean a state of complete nothingness. What appears there is happiness called enlightenment.

The perfect tranquility of nirvana is neither a negative state of mind nor a desire to escape reality. What you will find after being freed from attachment is the essence of enlightenment or the true nature of a human being. It is joy and true happiness; it is what humanity has long been searching for.

I have explained emptiness in relation to the Three Dharma Seals. Emptiness includes such meanings.

4

The Idea of Emptiness That Leads to Mahayana Thought

The idea of emptiness is said to be the core concept of Mahayana Buddhism, and I would like to discuss the reason for this here.

One reason is that the original text of the Prajna-paramita Sutra (the Perfection of Wisdom Sutra), which was composed of vast texts, was later made into a shorter version (usually called the Heart Sutra) containing only 262 Chinese characters. Because it is easier to read, all of the Mahayana Buddhist schools began to widely study the Heart Sutra.

Looking at the scriptures used by the Mahayana schools, we can see that the idea of emptiness is obviously central to their teachings.

Another reason is that this idea is not so relevant to the Hinayana approach—which attached much importance to the individual pursuit of enlightenment—but it is an extremely important way of thinking in Mahayana Buddhism in terms of its salvation standpoint.

On hearing the word emptiness, you may take it to be negative or nihilistic. You may think that life is meaningless, that this world is barren, or that there is nothing you can do but return to the other world. You may even think that there is no afterlife or that souls do not exist and sooner or later everything will disappear. But such thinking would eventually arrive at the idea that emptiness is the vanishing of all things—that extinction is the aim of life. It would turn into complete nihilism. But this is by no means the true meaning of emptiness.

As I have said before, emptiness does not mean denying all that exists. It implies the existence of *something*, but this *something* is not solid like an object that is visible in the three-dimensional world. It is not something concrete or substantial; it is transient and changing. Furthermore, this change is not only occurring in this three-dimensional world but also includes the transmigration between this world and the other world.

Therefore, although people questioned whether life continues after death or not, it is said in Buddhist studies that Shakyamuni Buddha did not give an answer to that question.

After all, a human being is not just a lump of flesh or a soul that has the fixed shape of a human form. Even the soul changes form, and this is why Buddha did not simply answer yes.

What kind of changes do we experience? The soul is made up of many different layers. First is the astral body, which is of the same size and form as the physical body and made of a substance very similar to matter. Beneath this is the spirit body, then the light body, and so on. As you can see, the human spirit is made up of several types of bodies, not just one. After returning to the other world, the different layers are gradually cast off one by one from the outside, and the soul changes form. The last thing that remains after all the layers have been cast off is a person's will or thoughts—in other words, the mind.

Ultimately, only the spiritual energy that has the ability to think remains. This is not a soul in the form of a physical human body; only the thinking energy remains.

This is what I mean by "emptiness is existence."

The last thing that remains of emptiness is purposeful spiritual energy. Once you break down a human being to this point, then you can say it exists. However, it is no longer in a form we can see. This is why it is difficult to simply answer yes or no when asked about the existence of life after death.

This is the beginning of ontology from the standpoint of the Middle Way.

5

Salvation and the Wonder of Existence Achieved through True Emptiness

I have said that the idea of emptiness leads to salvation, but this may still be difficult for people to understand, so let me continue to explain further.

If we look at emptiness from the Hinayana perspective, it is a highly effective idea that leads people to eliminate attachment. If you were pursuing your own happiness only—in other words, seeking your own enlightenment only—then you would probably be satisfied and stop at that point.

However, if you see all things as empty and if nihilism or complete nothingness appears after letting go of everything, this is a far cry from salvation or the Mahayana standpoint. This is when you must look beyond nihilism to see what lies behind it. There, you will find great energy or life force springing up in everything. This is the point where emptiness develops into the Mahayana movement.

What it means is that emptiness does not mean nothingness. Understanding the idea of emptiness means seeing through to the Light of Buddha or seeing the Energy of Buddha behind all things. If you see yourself as a manifestation of the Energy of Buddha and see all things and living beings in this world as different manifestations of the Energy of Buddha, this gives rise to a very positive worldview. Although the original meaning of emptiness was a denial of worldly ways of seeing and thinking, further exploration of this denial will make you realize that there is powerful life energy within all things—that life itself exists deep within everything.

This realization is expressed in Buddhism as "all living beings have Buddha-nature within" (from the Nirvana Sutra).

Buddha-nature means the Energy or Will of Buddha that allows all living beings to continue to live.

Therefore, usually you are filled with worldly, everyday thoughts, such as *I*, *you*, *this dog*, and *that cat*, but when you firmly deny such thoughts by seeing emptiness in all things, you will come to see how the compassion of Buddha manifests in all the things of this world.

You will then perceive the inexpressibly exquisite flavor of enlightenment in this new perspective of the world. After transcending the simple affirmation or denial of reality, you will see a wonderful world coming into focus before you. In old terms, this is known as *the wonder of existence achieved through true emptiness*. When you truly experience emptiness, you will see the exquisite existences out of this world.

Attaining emptiness is not the same as becoming nothing. When you awaken to true emptiness, there appears a wonderful reality before you.

In the Buddhist tradition, the state of this wonderful reality and wonderful world appearing before you is called achieving the *wonders of existences* (*myo-u*). This is in fact the grand starting point of Mahayana.

When you leave behind all attachments, the Mercy of Buddha appears before you in the form of all living beings. As all things are manifestations of Buddha's Mercy, you will see that you must do away with the narrow-minded notion of self-preservation. The wish to love others arises, as well as the desire to cooperate with others in striving to build Utopia, Buddha Land.

In fact, I believe this idea of the wonder of existence achieved through true emptiness is an extremely important viewpoint of how Hinayana developed into Mahayana with emptiness as the keyword.

This is indeed the thinking that connects emptiness to salvation. When individuals depart from their attachments and when they discover that all existences are good in nature, a spring of energy appears and spreads the goodness of all things even more.

6

Offerings and the Three Pure Wheels

When thinking further about this standpoint of salvation, there comes another point that we mustn't forget.

That is the act of giving—in other words, making offerings. Buddhism has long taught the merit and importance of making offerings, but what makes an offering truly precious and meaningful? Let us consider this in relation to the idea of emptiness.

Although making an offering is certainly an act of giving, the simple act of giving material objects, such as giving a dog a bone, cannot be considered the goal of making offerings. In Buddhism, it is said that the act of making an offering contributes to the development of the soul and to the building of Buddha Land on earth. If this is the case, there must be certain conditions for making offerings. The noble act of making an offering should not be the simple transfer of material objects or money; there has to be a noble spirit behind it.

According to Buddhist tradition, the three pure wheels are the prerequisites for making an offering.

Unless these three wheels are pure and clean, the offering you make will not be acceptable. The three wheels here refer to the giver, the receiver, and the object of offering (this not only refers to material objects but also includes the teachings). To make an offering meaningful, these three wheels have to be pure and free of defilement.

Defilement here means attachment or impurity.

At times, when you give something to someone, you may do so reluctantly. For example, there are people who give money unwillingly; they do so because other people push them into doing it, but deep down, they don't really want to give it away. And there are people who give money to beggars, pretending to be charitable, while in their hearts they despise the receivers. So people sometimes give things reluctantly, remaining attached to the thing they are giving, or they may be giving out of vanity.

In such cases, the giver's mind is impure, so there cannot be any merit in the offering.

On the other hand, if the person who is receiving has a selfish desire or an impure thought, then in this case too, there is no merit in the offering.

For instance, there are plenty of people who raise funds on the pretext that it will be used to help underprivileged children, when in fact they are going to use it for other purposes. It is often reported that canned foods sent to help save refugees in developing countries do not reach their destination and instead get sold elsewhere. There are cases of such aids going to the wrong place and ending up being goods for the market.

This kind of donation or offering is meaningless, so the attitude on the receiver's side is also of concern.

Therefore, those who are giving must do so with a pristine mind with no complaints or attachments, and those who are receiving offerings must do so with a heart of gratitude and the feeling of wanting to utilize it preciously. In this way, both sides must be without egoistic desires.

Last, the object of offering should also be pure. Objects that have been stolen, that are of doubtful origin, or that are unsuitable for offering are not considered acceptable.

Regarding the object of offering, let me touch on the Buddhist tradition regarding eating meat.

It is commonly thought that Buddhism prohibits eating meat, but this is a misunderstanding. Originally, Buddhism did not deny the eating of meat; what it did forbid was eating the kind of meat considered inappropriate as an offering. Such meat was called "meat that has been seen, heard, or suspected," and the monks and nuns were prohibited from eating these three kinds of meat.

If the monks or nuns had seen an animal, such as a pig or boar, being killed in front of them, they had to refrain from eating its meat. It meant that such meat was inappropriate for monks.

Second, if they had heard that the animal was killed for them, then they must refuse the offering. In other words, if they heard that a rabbit, for example, had just been killed to be given to them, they had to refuse to eat it. ("Heard" is sometimes referred to as hearing the voices of animals being killed, but this definition would not be so different from that of "seen." Therefore, I have understood this in a broad sense.)

Last, they had to refrain from eating any meat that was suspected to be the meat from an animal that had just been killed for them. Let's say that a whole pig was offered by lay followers saying that it was something that they happened to have. But if the monks cannot believe it and suspect that the animal had just been killed specifically to make offerings to them, then they had to refuse to eat the meat.

The reason these three kinds of meat were prohibited from being eaten was that animals, too, have souls; when they are killed, they feel pain. So it is against the essential nature of spiritual discipline for monks and nuns to cause pain to animals on their own account.

The purpose of the spiritual discipline of monks and nuns is to guide others in returning to heaven after death, so they have to refrain from actions that would prevent other living beings from attaining peace of mind.

This is why it was prohibited to eat these three kinds of meat that had been seen, heard, or suspected. All other kinds of meat were called undefiled meat, and they were allowed to eat these.

When the monks and nuns went on their daily rounds to receive alms, laypeople put various foods into their bowls. The food they were given was sometimes specially prepared for them; at other times, they were leftovers. Because laypeople ate meat, the food offered to them often had meat. Of course, the monks and nuns could not pick out the meat and throw it away; they had to eat all the food that was offered. So they ate all kinds of meat except for the ones that were suspected to be the three kinds of prohibited meat. Since the time of Shakyamuni Buddha, religious practitioners have been eating meat.

Therefore, it is not true to say that Buddhism totally prohibits the eating of meat or that the monks and nuns in Shakyamuni's time ate only Buddhist cuisine, which is vegetarian or vegan food. This habit began years later, after the rise of Mahayana Buddhism.

So far, I have talked about the objects of offering, which should be pure and undefiled. Monks and nuns were prohibited from eating meat that was considered defiled, but everything else was accepted as a precious offering.

When a monk saw a layman about to give him something he could not accept, it was customary for the monk to turn his bowl over, which signified refusal. As long as he was holding out his bowl, he had to take all that was put into it. In principle, monks and nuns were not allowed to complain no matter what sort of food they were given. When they thought they could not accept food, they turned their bowl over and silently left the house of those laypeople.

7

Emptiness and Love That Gives

The spirit of offering I have just described actually refers to *love that gives* (mercy), which is one of the most important teachings of Happy Science.

When you practice such love, you have to check to see if you have any impure thoughts such as a selfish desire or the desire for fame, vanity, or material objects. You must make sure the three pure wheels are satisfied.

Here, too, the idea of emptiness is very important. In other words, you must let go of all attachments when you are giving. You must abandon your attachment to everything.

In reality, there is neither *I* nor an object of offering. All things are manifestations of the great Mercy of Buddha changing form and being moved from one place to another. So you must not become attached to things such as food or money. When you make an offering, give with an empty heart. When you are on the receiving side, do not have any selfish desires; receive the offering with an empty heart. It is important in both cases that you also see the object of offering as essentially empty. (This is called the three empty wheels.)

Sometimes you may give others money, status, or honor in the name of love that gives, but if you do so expecting some return or with the mind of give-and-take, then in the eyes of the Truth, your giving becomes valueless because it will be impure.

Therefore, in the cycle of giving love, where love is circulating from one person to another, do not forget the idea of emptiness.

After all, from the perspective of salvation, I can say the following: because an understanding of emptiness leads to the realization of the existence of Buddha-nature in all living beings and the wonder of existence achieved through true emptiness, it can be used a positive principle for action in this world. The idea of emptiness is also essential in making an offering as an act of salvation.

Professional monks do not usually make offerings of material objects; their offering is to preach the Dharma to others. In this case, too, the three pure wheels should be observed.

It is important to always check for anything impure in the mind of the person preaching the Law and for any impure thoughts in the minds of those who come to listen to the teachings. There is also a question of whether the teachings themselves are not contaminated or contain something impure. Check to see whether the Law itself includes the desire for self-recognition, contains the wrong teachings, or contains an interpretation convenient for one's self-interest.

So when you practice giving love in your everyday life, ask yourself if you are giving in the spirit of offering. Always check that the three wheels—the giver, the receiver, and the object of offering—are pure and without defilement. In this way, there is still room for you to apply the idea of emptiness more and more carefully in your daily practice of giving love.

CHAPTER FIVE

Egolessness from the Perspective of the Middle Way

1

The Idea of Egolessness and Its Misinterpretation in Later Times

In this chapter, I would like to continue from Part One, Chapter Four, and talk on the topic of egolessness. This is because there is a major problem with this theme that very much concerns the basic philosophy of Buddhism.

In India, during Shakyamuni's time, a group of about 30 young men went out on a picnic one day with their wives to enjoy eating, drinking, and singing in the woods. Among them was a man much younger than the rest of them, who was still unmarried, and he brought with him a prostitute.

However, while they were all having a good time drinking, the prostitute took their money and precious jewels and ran away. Naturally, all of the young men became angry and ran after the woman, but in the course of their pursuit, they came across a *sramana* meditating alone in the woods. Sramana refers to an ascetic living alone in the forest while undergoing spiritual discipline in search of enlightenment. Usually, ascetics were free and renounced seekers of *Kshatriya*, the royal or warrior class, not Brahmin, the priest class.

The young men asked the sramana if he had seen the woman. The sramana came out of meditation and slowly opened his eyes. Then, he replied, "Young ones, what are you planning to do with the woman?" They answered, "She ran off with our money. We are here in the woods to search around for her and help our friend."

The sramana then said to the young men, "Now, which do you think is more valuable, searching for a woman or searching for yourself?"

They fell silent for a moment and then answered, "It's more valuable to search for one's own self." Hearing this, the sramana said, "Well, young ones, sit down here. I will preach the Dharma for you." Then, he talked about the Truth at length in a manner that was easy for them to understand.

Listening to the teachings, the young men had their picnic mood swept out of their minds; they eventually shaved their heads to become the disciples of this sramana.

The sramana was none other than Gautama Buddha, Shakyamuni. Shakyamuni asked them straightforwardly, "To search and seek for a woman or to search and seek for one's own self—which one is superior? Which one of them is more important for you?" In other words, Buddha himself talked about the importance of searching for one's own self. This is a historical fact found in one of the Buddhist scriptures, *Vinaya-pitaka* (*Dharmaguptaka vinaya*, vol.32 and *Mahisasaka vinaya*, vol.15), which means "a collection of precepts."

Nonetheless, a completely opposite idea is found within the common philosophy of egolessness. In later times, some began to insist that because Buddha taught egolessness, the self was to be denied or totally extinguished.

Religion, however, is a path of discipline for seeking enlightenment, so the self should always be explored. Obviously, there is something wrong with the view that the self should be extinguished. If this were true, there would be no room for any discussion on self-discipline.

This mistaken view appeared 200 to 300 years after the passing of Shakyamuni Buddha, when several groups of monks and nuns, now classified as Hinayana Buddhists (those in early Buddhist schools), made an extensive study of the teachings of Buddha. Among them was a group called *Sarvastivada*, which means "existence school[6]." After studying Buddha's idea of egolessness, they concluded that there was no such entity as the "ego" in the form of a soul and that a human being was but a temporary composite of the five aggregates—matter, feeling, perception, volition, and consciousness.

Matter means the physical body; *feeling* refers to the functioning of the senses; *perception* is the forming of images or ideas; *volition* is the power of will that puts an idea or image into action; and *consciousness* is the ability to recognize or understand.

They thought that a human being was made up of these five aspects of the mind and body. They believed that nothing but these functions made up a human being.

But what would happen if we were to delve further into this thinking? You can see how that would eventually be quite similar to how you dissect a frog and apply an electric shock to its nervous system to observe muscle contractions.

It seems that the early Buddhists tried to analyze the various sensory and mental functions of human beings based on materialistic thoughts. Therefore, they gave up on exploring what is behind and beyond those human functions.

So the existence school of Hinayana Buddhism advocated the theory of egolessness as "there is no spiritual self" and interpreted human beings merely as a temporary composite of five aggregates. Since then, in the history of Buddhist philosophy, discussions on egolessness have become complicated and difficult to understand.

2

Shakyamuni Buddha's True Intention

It is indeed true that Shakyamuni taught the idea of egolessness and that it was one of the markers of Buddhism.

In India, prior to Buddhism, there was a traditional religion called Brahminism, which taught the oneness of Brahma and atman. *Brahma* is a divine being who resides in heaven, whereas *atman* means the central core of a spiritual body that resides within an individual (back then, people assumed that a soul was about the size of a thumb). Brahminism taught that although the atman within each individual seemed to be a different entity from the god-like being called Brahma, essentially, they were one and the same. (In other words, the individual and the laws of the universe were essentially the same.) They thought that after a person died and returned to heaven, the soul (atman) of each individual would become one with the great divine spirit (Brahma), just like how the water molecules of a river flow into and become one with the great ocean. What is more, they thought that atman was the very part of a human being that goes through reincarnation.

Then, Buddhism appeared as a new philosophy that criticized this theory of ego; it said that Brahminism had stagnated and that monks had neglected their disciplines and become corrupt. Because Buddhism emerged with this intention of criticizing the traditional religion, its doctrines tended to be misinterpreted as opposing the theories of Brahminism that affirmed the existence of the self.

However, the idea of egolessness that Shakyamuni Buddha preached was not intended to be taken as a denial of the existence of the self. He wanted to say, "Because selfish desires are the cause of suffering, unless those desires are abandoned, there can be no happiness. The root cause of human desire is ego-consciousness, so when ego-consciousness is abandoned, happiness can be attained. Try to eliminate the ego-consciousness that is the root cause of desire."

Egolessness was therefore taught as a way to control the mind; it was not meant to be taken as a total denial of the existence of the self or ego. Buddha taught that in order to eliminate the suffering that arises from the self, it is necessary to meditate, discipline the mind, and become selfless. He taught egolessness as a method, not as a denial of the existence of the self.

However, you may all well understand that a shallow comprehension can lead to misunderstandings such as whether something exists or not. And the reality is that many people still have the tendency to understand this idea in such a way. This shows that in the end, it all comes down to whether you can believe in spiritual beings and the existence of the other world.

Therefore, Buddhism became one of the academic fields and gradually turned into a pile-up of worldly knowledge, so people could no longer understand such things.

Among scholars of religion are quite a few atheists and materialists. Although they are professionals in the religious field, they cannot believe in the other world, which means there is a fundamental problem with their view of life. For those who cannot surpass this borderline and believe in the spiritual, their argument will be nothing but an opinion on paper. The theory of the existence school that denied the existence of the self as an entity influenced the philosophy of Mahayana Buddhism in its early stages, and this mistaken view has been passed down to this day. Because of this, even today, many say that because Buddhism advocates egolessness, it denies the existence of the soul and the other world.

If you read the Buddhist scriptures very carefully, however, you will find that there are many stories that do not make sense without admitting the existence of the other world and the soul. If the other world did not exist, how could the scriptures talk of returning to heaven? Without a belief in the other world, how could they talk about Amitabha

Buddha? If it were not for the other world, how could there be stories about living peacefully in heaven or falling to hell? If there was no such thing as the reincarnation of the soul, how could Buddha have repeatedly taught about the seven Buddhas of the past, which were his own past lives[7]?

Furthermore, when Shakyamuni Buddha preached the Law to laypeople, he often used the method of "step-by-step teaching," which began by teaching easy content and led up to advanced teachings. He first talked about a set of three different practices—making offerings, observing the precepts, and returning to heaven. He recommended people make offerings and observe the precepts and assured them that they would be able to return to heaven if they undertook these practices sincerely. It is hard to believe that Shakyamuni Buddha—the one who taught that a seeker of enlightenment must not tell lies—would make up a story as an expedient to teach people about offerings and precepts.

When you connect the dots, you can see how the existence of the other world and the existence and reincarnation of souls were naturally included in Shakyamuni's teachings.

But those who can only understand these concepts as a metaphor, story, or literature cannot believe in such spiritual things. That is why they can only think analytically.

I can understand why they think that way. In modern Western philosophy, analytical thinking is the mainstream; it analyzes and explores human mentality without having any idea as to whether or not the other world and the soul actually exist. This may be ignorance that comes with humans living in a physical body.

In summary, what Shakyamuni Buddha intended to teach was the importance of abandoning the selfish desires that arise out of the ego derived from the physical body, which cause suffering. Egolessness was taught to make people aware of the importance of eliminating attachment, but in later times, this idea was warped into a philosophy that denied the existence of the self or ego as an entity. Such misunderstanding occurred in the history of Buddhism.

3

Reasons for the Decline of Buddhism in India

As a result of the misinterpretation of egolessness, or the idea that there is no physical self as an entity, that appeared in Hinayana Buddhism, there naturally arose the question, "Then, what about reincarnation?" Reincarnation itself was not necessarily the core philosophy of Shakyamuni; in other words, it was not his original idea, but back then, in India, the concept of reincarnation was accepted by the majority and Buddhism also acknowledged it.

Later, some people began to question how reincarnation was possible if there was no self or ego. Because everyone believed in reincarnation, Buddhists had difficulty explaining this point.

Naturally, some of the other Indian religions such as Brahminism and its popular, everyday faith called Hinduism began to criticize Buddhism by saying, "If the existence of the self is denied, how can there be reincarnation?" "If everything disappears after death, there can be no reincarnation, so the Buddhist philosophy must be wrong."

Because Buddhists received such criticism and were troubled by it, they had to come up with theoretical arguments to defend themselves. Because they taught egolessness, they could not talk about the soul. So they had to replace the idea of the soul with something else.

Then, one of the Buddhist schools, the Consciousness-Only school, began to present the idea of *consciousness* in place of the soul. According to the new theory, several levels of consciousness existed in the mind. First were the six different kinds of consciousness corresponding to the six sensory organs—namely, the eyes, the ears, the nose, the tongue, the tactile body, and the mind. Next, there was an inner level called manas-consciousness, and even deeper was a level called alaya-consciousness. So there were a total of eight different levels of consciousness, and alaya-consciousness was in fact the main subject that underwent reincarnation. In other words, they worked hard and, without using the word *soul*, established the theory that a deep subconscious level called *alaya* was the subject of reincarnation. They finally came up with it here.

To tell the truth, there was no need for Buddhists to go through the trouble of creating such a theory because Shakyamuni Buddha had never denied the reincarnation of the soul. However, because the *Abhidharma* (literary study of Shakyamuni's teachings) was established as an academic discipline in Hinayana, Buddhism became a philosophical study and caused later followers much trouble.

Many different schools were founded, such as the Consciousness-Only school, and they presented various theories to try and make the philosophy consistent. But it was actually the misinterpretation of egolessness that caused the inconsistencies and distorted the original teachings of Shakyamuni Buddha. This became one of the major causes of the decline of Buddhism in India.

There are several reasons why Buddhism virtually died out in India. One was the invasion of Islam that occurred in the 12th and 13th centuries. Muslims destroyed most of the Buddhist temples and massacred the monks and nuns[8].

Because Buddhism at that time was mainly upheld by the monks and nuns who had renounced secular life, there was no one left to pass on the teachings. One reason for the decline of Buddhism was the violent destruction caused by the Muslims.

Another reason for the decline was that Buddhism failed to be integrated into the lives and customs of the people. Whereas Hinduism was incorporated into people's daily lives, with its services for ceremonial occasions, Buddhism was rather a philosophical and academic study; so when the scriptures were burned and the monks and nuns were killed, nothing remained. In short, Buddhism hadn't been rooted deep enough in the land of India.

On the other hand, Hinduism was also involved in other activities such as funerals and weddings; in Japan, these would be equivalent to Buddhist funerals or Shinto weddings. Indian Buddhism did not reach out to such areas of life and instead stayed as a professional group of people who focused on studying the teachings. For that reason, Buddhism was exterminated by the invasion of Islam. However, despite the Islamic invasion, Hinduism survived because it was part of people's lives. People's lifestyles cannot be denied, and the entire nation cannot be killed, so that was why Hinduism survived. Buddhism died out because it did not play a big enough role in people's lives.

These two reasons have generally been given as the main causes of the decline of Buddhism, but the fundamental reason lies in the misinterpretation of egolessness. This error had turned Buddhism into a philosophy that could be mistaken for a form of materialism, and because of this, it conflicted with the concept of reincarnation, a fundamental belief most Indians upheld.

At that time, everyone believed in reincarnation. And without the soul, there can be no reincarnation. The teachings of Buddhism shifted from Shakyamuni's original intent at some point in history and could no longer clearly explain the soul. I presume that this flaw in logic eventually contributed to the decline of Buddhism.

Therefore, the teachings must be studied with much attention, as misinterpretations will have a great influence on future generations. Even if you explain in a philosophical, intellectual, or materialistic way to help people who don't believe in the other world to understand, when such an approach becomes the mainstream and the fundamental teachings are lost, the doctrine itself or the religion itself may end with its own destruction, as we have seen in the case in India.

In contrast, the Buddhism which later traveled to China and Japan has survived to this day. This is because it has been successfully integrated into the lives of the people, with services for ceremonial occasions, and the existence of the soul was taken to be a matter of course.

In China, Buddhism incorporated the various teachings of Taoism, the indigenous religions, as well as Confucianism, and it survived in a form quite different from the original Buddhism.

A way of understanding the teachings of Buddhism was developed by making comparisons with classical Chinese philosophies. This type of Buddhism is called "concept-matching" Buddhism. For example, it would mean trying to understand the concept of emptiness in the Prajna-paramita Sutra by comparing it with the Taoist philosophy of nothingness.

As Buddhism spread from China to Japan, it incorporated Japanese Shinto and was integrated into the lives of the people—for example, it placed importance on memorial services for ancestors. This is how Buddhism changed to survive through the times.

We are currently living now, so the future is somewhat uncertain, but what is important is to learn from the past. I believe that at least we must first learn from history and then further build upon our current way of thinking.

4

A Major Correction to Buddhist Studies

From my explanation so far, you must have understood why I am focusing on egolessness as a matter of great significance.

As I have said, if we take egolessness to be a question of whether or not the self physically exists rather than a question of how to control the mind, this will eventually lead to the self-destruction of religion. That is why I am saying that this very point must never be mistaken.

What I am saying is in fact a fairly significant correction to Buddhist studies.

Shakyamuni Buddha had a clear idea that the self should be refined and developed. It should always be explored; only when it is explored can there be a way to becoming a bodhisattva or a tathagata. Climbing these stairs toward the state of buddhahood is the path of spiritual discipline for human beings. This was Shakyamuni's idea; so strictly speaking, the subject of spiritual discipline was the self.

The law of cause and effect is one of the basic teachings of Buddhism, and it leads to the principle of accepting responsibility for what one has done. But if it were not for the soul as the subject that takes responsibility, there could be no such principle in the first place. I believe this is an aspect that must not be forgotten.

In the end, the idea of egolessness must be understood in the following way: if you explore the depths of human unhappiness in this world, you will find that the root cause lies in desires that come from the physical body. So we have to review the ego-consciousness that arises from the physical body.

This ego-consciousness manifests, for example, as the Three Poisons of the Mind—greed, anger, and foolishness.

Greed is desire itself. Desire comes from worldly thoughts and mostly has to do with the physical body. There are many kinds of desires, such as those arising from the eyes, ears, nose, tongue, hands, and feet or from internal organs. Suffering is born from various desires—namely, bodily desires.

Another example is anger. Animals are quick to bare their teeth and become angry. If you are quick to fly into a rage or are short-tempered, then this proves that you have animalistic tendencies. Animals quickly bare their teeth, show their claws, or raise their quill to protect themselves from danger. In fact, humans have such animalistic characteristics.

Foolishness is, to put it in another way, ignorance. There are many people who do foolish things and cause their own suffering simply because they do not know the Truth. For instance, although wise people can anticipate that walking through a puddle will soil their shoes (doing bad deeds will harm their souls), those who are unwise cannot imagine what will happen until they have actually stepped into the puddle. Such kinds of incidents happen countless times. Even among religious scholars, foolish people criticize authentic religions and support misguided ones. There are people who lack wisdom, although they may be well-educated. These three are delusions and suffering that come with living in this world.

In addition, there are pride and doubt.

Pride here means a sense of superiority that comes from comparing one's own abilities with those of others and judging them based on worldly values without being aware of the infinitely great being, such as Buddha or God. Some people think themselves superior to others. Even when they meet a person who is far superior, they think the person is no different from themselves; or they think that someone whose state of mind is much closer to Buddha than their own is just an ordinary human being like themselves.

About 2,000 years ago, in Israel, there were people who saw Jesus Christ and yet could not believe he was the savior. They thought he was just the son of a carpenter and saw him only through human eyes until the end. Two thousand years later, ironically, people worship the image of Jesus on the cross. This is another example of pride.

Then there is doubt. At the core of all doubts is doubt about the Three Treasures: Buddha, Dharma, and Sangha. Some make this mistake because their values are only based on worldly or physical values; they cannot believe in the unseen.

And there is wrong view. There are actually many kinds of wrong views, so let me name some typical ones.

One is what could be called physical view. This is a way of seeing things that is centered on the physical body. Those who see in this way believe themselves to be no more than physical beings.

Next, there is extreme view. For example, some people think that everything ends at the time of death, whereas others think that everything will continue as it is, even after death.

There is yet another wrong view called evil view. It involves having wrong religious beliefs—those who believe in a misguided religion or those involved in it. In Shakyamuni's time, people who did not believe in the law of cause and effect were considered those with evil view.

The law of cause and effect specifically means that bad acts lead to bad results, whereas good acts lead to good results. If you do something good, you will be able to return to heaven, and if you do something bad, you will go to hell. The law of cause and effect is a basic principle, but many people are still unable to think in such a way. Some are materialists who think that everything ends with death, whereas others think that there is no cause and effect and that human beings can act freely and do whatever they like. These mistaken religious beliefs, such as epicurean or fatalist views, are classified as evil views.

There is also another kind of people who think, "What is the point of self-discipline? It is of no use making any effort. It serves humans no good." Others think, "The idea of creating utopia is a lie. It's just a way of tricking people. What is the use of the idea of realizing Buddha Land? We are better off thinking about how to get something to eat and drink today." These kinds of perspectives that go against the ideals are all called evil views.

In Buddhism, greed, anger, foolishness, pride, doubt, and wrong view are also called the Six Worldly Delusions. These are the representatives of human desires. "Worldly delusion" is a general term for the negative workings of the mind or the false beliefs that make people unhappy.

These Six Worldly Delusions mostly stem from a physical view of life that recognizes one's physical body as oneself, the view that life is limited to this world only.

Unless these delusions are eliminated, one cannot attain true happiness. That is why you should deny the ego-consciousness of the physical body—the origin of worldly delusion. This is the idea of egolessness.

5

Egolessness from the Perspective of the Middle Way

While it is important to deny the ego based on a physical view, it is also important to pursue the true or spiritual self, the self that seeks to become one with Buddha, which is something to be polished. Your true self must progress toward Buddha. In this way, the self is something to be polished, something that must make progress.

To make things clear, it could be said that whereas the *ego* should be denied, the *self* should be explored and developed. The self indeed exists (the Sanskrit word *atman* means both the self and the ego).

Therefore, you must not mistake this point. You may think there is a simple "yes or no" answer to whether or not the ego or the self exists. But in the world of Truth, the ego should be denied, whereas the true self should be refined and developed. These two directions may appear to contradict each other, but they can be integrated into one coherent theory if seen from a higher point of view.

"It is not just about whether it exists or not. It is something to be denied and, at the same time, something to be affirmed and developed." This was the central point of what Shakyamuni wanted to say.

Egolessness is an idea that denies the ego centered on the physical body and, at the same time, affirms the existence of the true self as something that should be developed. So inherent in this idea are both denial and affirmation; it is not about inclining to either path but a way of thinking to develop and grow the self by considering both paths. Here you can see the way to development.

After all, both theories of simply affirming and denying the existence of the ego are extreme views. You must understand that Shakyamuni Buddha's true intention lies in the Middle Way, away from either path. In this way, egolessness can be interpreted from the viewpoint of the Middle Way. We can call this *the theory of egolessness from the perspective of the Middle Way*.

No matter how much you develop and expand the ego-consciousness that comes from the physical body, you will not achieve true happiness or true growth. Therefore, such a view must be denied. However, infinitely polishing and developing the spiritual self, the self that is a part of Buddha, will lead you to true happiness. This is something that must be developed.

The idea of egolessness is, therefore, not a one-sided view but a crucial philosophy that helps you to grow and make progress through the Middle Way while actually being aware of your true self.

To put it simply, egolessness is an idea that teaches you to become as pure and transparent as possible. Because the human mind tends to be clouded by impurities, like a windowpane covered in dust or dirt, you must clean it thoroughly and render it crystal clear. Then, make efforts to develop your pure, transparent self.

To become pure and transparent does not mean you extinguish your being. You clear away the clouds or impurities, but you do not get rid of your existence.

The point is, the idea of egolessness is not the advice to crush yourself to bits and kill yourself but to make yourself become clear like a crystal.

Make the crystal clear and encourage it to grow and become more beautiful. That is the idea of egolessness from the perspective of the Middle Way, as well as the idea of progress through the Middle Way.

CHAPTER SIX

Buddha-Nature and Buddhahood

1

Buddha-Nature and Stored Tathagata

In this chapter, I have chosen the theme "Buddha-Nature and Buddhahood." This theme cannot be thoroughly explained in just one chapter. However, these concepts are very important, and inherent in them is a very significant problem that we at Happy Science should not overlook.

As the term suggests, *Buddha-nature* means the nature of Buddha. I have also previously explained its meaning in many other lectures—for instance, "It is the nature of all human beings as children of Buddha," "Everyone is a diamond," and "The souls of all living creatures such as plants, animals, and humans originally split off from the Light of Buddha." What I have consistently taught is that at the core of all living beings is the energy of Buddha's Light. So the term Buddha-nature is quite familiar among the members of Happy Science.

In Buddhism, *stored tathagata* is often used as a synonym for Buddha-nature. In this case, "stored" does not simply mean being kept at a storehouse or warehouse. The original Sanskrit term is *tathagata-garbha*; *garbha* means embryo. So this term literally means "an embryo of tathagata."

It implies that people are not yet full-fledged tathagata or buddha; they are just like an embryo in the mother's womb, but if they grow and develop, they can become tathagata. Everyone has this potential.

This idea became very popular among Buddhists in India because they were delighted to hear that they were a tathagata-to-be.

When this word reached China, it was translated into stored tathagata and therefore came to have a slightly different meaning. Although the original meaning was an embryo of tathagata, the Chinese took it to mean that a tathagata is covered and cannot be seen. This was apparently because of the way in which the term was translated, implying that tathagata lay hidden in a storehouse, like a grain of rice inside the husk.

The meaning had changed from an embryo to something that is covered and hidden or wrapped up. However, the original meaning is an embryo of tathagata, as mentioned before, and back then, this term was almost synonymous with Buddha-nature.

Now, where did the idea of stored tathagata come from?

As I have explained in Part Two, Chapter Four, in the Nirvana Sutra, we find the phrase "all living beings have Buddha-nature within." Oftentimes, "all living beings" refers to human beings, so you can take this phrase to mean "all human beings have Buddha-nature within them."

Of the scriptures that remain to this day, the idea of Buddha-nature first appeared in the Nirvana Sutra. Here is where the idea comes from—that Buddha-nature resides in all living beings or, in other words, all human beings.

2

Icchantika: Incorrigible Disbelievers

The idea of Buddha-nature is indeed wonderful, but there is one problem with it: there are still people in the world who do not seem to be able to spiritually awaken, no matter how hard they try.

How to handle these real matters became the topic of a huge argument that developed into a long-standing debate that has been going on for hundreds of years. The reality is that we sometimes meet people who do not seem to have Buddha-nature.

For example, some people persecute authentic religions and their believers. Do these people have Buddha-nature too? Can they be considered potential tathagatas? There are also people who do not hinder the spreading of the Truth, but cannot understand the teachings at all when they listen to them; such people may seem incapable of attaining enlightenment. Then, there are others who have absolutely no interest in religion. These kinds of people exist in every age, a fact that has long been a great problem for Buddhists.

It is an extremely wonderful idea to say that all living beings have Buddha-nature. However, Buddhist scholars feared that this idea could be interpreted as follows: even those who persecuted Buddhist believers, criticized their teachings, or could not see the difference between Buddha and criminals ought to be considered equal to everyone else. This was a dilemma.

After struggling to solve this problem, they naturally came up with the idea that "although everyone has Buddha-nature within and possesses the potential for buddhahood, there are some whose root of good nature is completely nipped or who have no belief at all in God or Buddha. They are like floating weeds and are not connected to Buddha." They called these people *icchantika* in Sanskrit, which literally means "a person who can never be enlightened."

As we conduct religious activities for a long time, we sometimes meet people who seem too helpless. So although the Nirvana Sutra made a revolutionary claim that everyone has Buddha-nature, Buddhist scholars said there are exceptions to the rule, the exceptions being icchantika.

Historically, the word icchantika was used to refer to those who criticized Mahayana Buddhism. Buddhists denounced those who criticized them: "Although we teach that you too have Buddha-nature, you still criticize this great teaching. So you are out of the question. There is no hope for you to be enlightened."

In my view, however, everyone has an innate nature as a child of Buddha, no matter who they may be. Everyone smiles when they see a small child or feels happy when they meet someone they like. So I believe that everyone has the qualities of Buddha-nature such as love and compassion.

If a cocoon grows too hard, the silkworm will not be able to come out. Although a cocoon is originally made by the worldly delusions (threads) of a human being with Buddha-nature (silkworm), if the cocoon becomes too tough, you won't be able to take out what is inside. This is the state of icchantika. They have created such thick clouds of worldly desires or delusions.

Possession by evil spirits can also be an obstacle. People who are possessed by as many as four or five evil spirits can no longer make the right judgments. They cannot think of Buddha or God at all and criticize the teachings as if it is a matter of course. Oftentimes, it is not the people under possession but the possessing spirits who make such criticism.

Those people seem as though they have no chance of believing in the true teachings owing to the beliefs that have influenced them since birth, owing to the lessons gained from their education or occupation, or because of possession due to a mistaken mind. Yet I believe that they have Buddha-nature at their root. Nevertheless, we must accept the fact that some people do not appear to have Buddha-nature and act that way.

It is the same as how in Happy Science, I teach that no one living in this world is born from hell. Souls in hell must return to heaven before they can be reborn. In many other religions, however, they seem to think that about half the people come from heaven, whereas the other half come from hell. If we believe this, we will simply look at people as good or bad, and this will be a problem from the viewpoint of salvation.

Babies and small children are all beautiful and innocent. Although some may later go astray and become criminals or a part of a gang, not a single baby has such a tendency from the beginning.

Some babies may look grumpy, but none of them show such a brutal personality from age one, two, or three. It is something that surfaces later on. You should understand it in such a way.

So although sometimes you may meet people who seem as though their root of good nature is completely nipped, you need to be compassionate and know that they, too, have Buddha-nature at the core of their souls.

3

Innate Enlightenment and Acquired Enlightenment

As we have seen, the Buddhist theory that everyone has Buddha-nature within is invaluable teaching, but as it has been handed down through history, it has brought with it a serious problem—the clash between the ideas of "all living beings have Buddha-nature within" and "all living beings become a buddha."

The fact that everyone has Buddha-nature within means that everyone has the potential to attain buddhahood or the innate nature of tathagata deep within. But the question is whether this also means that everyone will actually achieve buddhahood.

Some say that as long as we have Buddha-nature within, we can all attain buddhahood. Others say, however, that although everyone possesses Buddha-nature, some can attain buddhahood whereas others cannot. These different thoughts turned into a big problem.

In Buddhism, this problem is known as the argument between *innate enlightenment* and *acquired enlightenment*. The philosophy of innate enlightenment states that because all human beings have Buddha-nature within, they were originally enlightened beings, or they were already enlightened before they were born into this world. The idea of innate enlightenment is known as the Tendai innate enlightenment philosophy in the Tendai schools of Buddhism. Tendai school, whose head temple is located on Mount Hiei, upholds this idea. It means that you are already an enlightened being.

On the contrary, the philosophy of acquired enlightenment asserts that human beings can attain enlightenment only after they have learned the teachings and undergone spiritual discipline.

When these two philosophies are put into an argument against each other, acquired enlightenment usually turns out less popular. According to the majority vote in superficial democracy, the majority would naturally prefer the idea, "You are all enlightened beings since birth, so all of you can become a tathagata." Only a few people would incline toward the idea, "Only those who succeed in spiritual discipline can become enlightened." Those who are not confident in attaining enlightenment would not prefer this idea. In this way, the innate enlightenment philosophy sounds more generous, so it is apt to be advantageous in an argument. Because this philosophy is more flattering and pleasing to everyone, most people will naturally be inclined toward innate enlightenment in a majority vote.

However, when we think about how Shakyamuni Buddha attained his great enlightenment through spiritual discipline, we have to admit that there is an obvious problem with innate enlightenment thinking. This can be a major subject of discussion in Buddhism.

4

The Debate between Saicho and Tokuitsu: One Vehicle Philosophy vs. Three Vehicles Philosophy

The debate between Saicho (767–822, the founder of the Tendai school) and Tokuitsu (ca. 749–824, a leading monk of the Hosso sect) was the great dispute between the two philosophies: innate enlightenment and acquired enlightenment. This was a debate regarding which was the true teaching—the one vehicle philosophy or the three vehicles philosophy.

The three vehicles philosophy states that there are three different categories of spiritual seekers: *hearers* (those who listen to the teachings), *solitary realizers* (those seeking enlightenment without a teacher's guidance), and bodhisattvas (those who devote themselves to saving others). Each of these groups has its own form of spiritual discipline. This philosophy accords with what has long been handed down by the Hinayana schools. This could be considered traditional Buddhist teaching, as it has been mentioned since Buddha was still alive.

In contrast, the one vehicle philosophy, represented by the Lotus Sutra, states that Buddha's description of the three different ways for seekers was a mere expedient. In fact, anyone can achieve buddhahood, and there should be only one vehicle, Buddha vehicle.

The term *Buddha vehicle* is sometimes referred to as *bodhisattva vehicle*. In Mahayana Buddhism, becoming a bodhisattva was considered the same as becoming a buddha. In the Mahayana movement, the goal of every follower was to become a bodhisattva: they were not interested in being categorized as hearers or solitary realizers. It is a movement where everyone aims to be a bodhisattva, which is the same as becoming a buddha. If we were to consider bodhisattva vehicle and Buddha vehicle as separate ideas, then it would no longer be the three vehicles but rather the four vehicles (the four vehicles that lead you to enlightenment—hearer vehicle, solitary realizer vehicle, bodhisattva vehicle, and Buddha vehicle). But Buddha vehicle and bodhisattva vehicle usually refer to the same idea.

Consequently, there has been much argument in the history of Buddhism about whether one vehicle or three vehicles was the correct teaching. In the Lotus Sutra, there is a section entitled Expedient Means, in which Shakyamuni Buddha says, "Sariputra, I have so far given various teachings, but to tell the truth, those teachings were all expedient means to help lead you to one understanding, that is, that everyone can become a buddha." On hearing this, everyone there was overjoyed to discover that they could all become buddha, as they thought they could only reach a level as high as a hearer.

There are also sections in the Lotus Sutra entitled "Bestowal of Prophecy" and "Prophecy of Enlightenment for Five Hundred Disciples," in which Shakyamuni Buddha assured many of his disciples that they too would be able to become a tathagata in the future.

This clearly shows how the Buddhist sects that were established hundreds of years after Shakyamuni Buddha's passing and had embraced the Lotus Sutra employed this one vehicle philosophy as a strategy to increase their followers. When they claimed that everyone could become a buddha, people were so delighted that the number of believers increased dramatically. I sense that such motives were at work. People in later days were not aware of how history unrolled, so they believed that all the Buddhist scriptures were Buddha's actual words and considered the one vehicle philosophy to be the true teaching. Therefore, they regarded the three vehicles philosophy simply as expediency and incorrect teaching.

When you pursue this idea further, it can lead to the innate enlightenment philosophy (claiming everyone was originally enlightened). Moreover, because they thought the idea that Buddha-nature existed in everyone was not satisfying enough, it was further developed into an extreme idea that everyone becomes a buddha.

But if this were the case, everyone would simply be treated as if they were all at the same spiritual level: those who practice spiritual discipline and those who don't, the novice seekers and the advanced seekers, and even the average person and historical greats such as Shakyamuni Buddha and Jesus Christ. Logically, that would be the case.

This is the reality in the world of politics. Under a democracy that is concerned with its formality, the rule is "one man, one vote," so everyone is equal. Whether people are executives or employees, whether they have studied hard or not, or whether they are a tathagata or a spirit in hell, everyone has one vote. Therefore, when you look at the philosophy of innate enlightenment in relation to political ideology, this religious idea appeared much earlier than the current political democracy. Although it appeared 1,000 or 2,000 years ago, it is the same idea as modern democracy—the idea of equality that says everyone is equal.

With such historical background, Saicho and Tokuitsu debated these two philosophies. Saicho advocated the one vehicle philosophy or the idea that Buddha-nature exists in all people, which later developed into the Tendai innate enlightenment philosophy. Tokuitsu, a prominent and knowledgeable monk and the representative of the Six

Schools of Nara Buddhism—the official Buddhism of the time—claimed that Saicho's theory was wrong and that Shakyamuni Buddha did not mean that, and he brought upon a debate with various points of argument.

Unfortunately, the only work of Tokuitsu remaining to this day is *Unresolved Matters Regarding Shingon*, so we can only piece together the debate by reading Saicho's works, which is not a fair way of judging the debate. Tokuitsu's arguments can only be taken up in excerpts from Saicho's work. However, as we read his works, it becomes obvious that Tokuitsu's attacks on Saicho were quite fierce and pointed out the flaws in his logic. You can see how Saicho made desperate counterarguments as he was in danger of losing his school.

For example, Tokuitsu wrote *On Buddha-Nature* (which also criticizes the works of T'ien-t'ai Chih-i, the founder of Chinese T'ien-t'ai Buddhism) to criticize Saicho's works, *The Basic Principles of Tendai* (in which Saicho advocates the one vehicle doctrine) and *Criticism On the Six- and Nine-Proof Essays Through Comparison* (in which Saicho criticized the ideas of "two vehicles of nature" and "sentient beings with no nature" that were written in *The Essentials of Consciousness-Only*, a work by the Hosso sect founder, Jion). Saicho refuted this with *The Mirror Illuminating the Provisional and the Real*. Tokuitsu also wrote *The Mirror on the Meaning of the Middle and the Extreme*, and Saicho refuted it with *Essays on Protecting the Nation*. After Tokuitsu wrote *The Mirror on the Meaning of the Middle and the Extreme*, *Wings and Feet Added to the Sun of Wisdom*, and *Shutting Out Heretical Opinions*, Saicho refuted them with *A Treatise on Discerning the Real from the Provisional* and *Precious Words on the Lotus Sutra*. The main argument of this debate had two points. One was about which teaching was true and which was expedient: one vehicle or three vehicles. The second was about the difference in their view of humans: "everyone can attain buddhahood" or "the Five Mutually Distinctive Natures" (see section 6).

This debate continued for years, until it was brought to an end by Saicho's death due to fatigue from the debate. In Saicho's last years, his dearest disciple Taihan, who was supposed to succeed him, left to become a disciple of Kukai. Out of Saicho's 24 disciples, only 10 remained, 6 converted to the Hosso sect, 7 left, and 1 died. Saicho died in such misery and complete distress.

Seven days after his death, however, his school was officially permitted by the state to set up a Mahayana ordination platform, and a new system of ordination started the following year. In those days, the formal ordination of monks and nuns could only be performed in Nara (the Hinayana ordination), but because that would be troublesome as Saicho was fighting against Nara Buddhism, he wanted to set up an independent ordination platform at Tendai head temple on Mt. Hiei. Unfortunately, this plan was not realized until after his death because the monks of Nara Buddhism strongly opposed it for fear of losing their power over the Tendai school. Saicho died in disappointment.

Ironically, the Tendai head temple on Mt. Hiei eventually flourished as a center of academic study, and because of this, the story of Saicho's debate with Tokuitsu was later passed down to say Saicho had the advantage. But the de facto reason for the loss of Nara Buddhism, to which Tokuitsu belonged, was that they could not produce powerful monks later on.

Meanwhile, in the Tendai school, after Saicho's death, the later disciples studied abroad in China to complement Saicho's teachings. They returned with volumes of new Buddhist teachings, which allowed the sect to flourish. Saicho was obviously not winning when he was still alive, but after prominent monks like Ennin (794-864) and Enchin (814-891), who studied abroad in China, brought back the new Buddhist philosophies and reformed the Tendai doctrine, the school became increasingly influential. As the Tendai school survived long after that, it came to be regarded as the orthodox school of Japanese Buddhism. Since then, the one vehicle philosophy became mainstream, whereas the three vehicles philosophy was considered heresy.

Many Japanese Buddhist sects that were established in the Kamakura period (1185–1333) also came under the influence of Tendai doctrine, so they advocated one vehicle as correct · and dismissed three vehicles as an outdated philosophy. In this way, naturally, their doctrines were based on the one vehicle philosophy. In time, Tokuitsu was forgotten and Saicho is remembered to this day as one of the most influential religious leaders of Japan.

5

Theoretical Buddha-Nature and Practical Buddha-Nature

Theoretically, however, it was Tokuitsu who was right. As I have often said, there are different levels or spiritual layers in the other world—the fourth, fifth, sixth, seventh, eighth, and ninth dimensions—and people are born into this world from the realm they belonged to in heaven; each person is at a different spiritual level. They have undergone different levels of spiritual discipline in their past lives, so when they are born into this world again, they undergo the corresponding level of spiritual discipline.

The place where people return to after death is usually at the same spiritual level as they were before being born. It is impossible that someone born from the fourth dimension will skip to the eighth dimension after death. For someone to reach the eighth dimension, they need to have undergone a very long period of spiritual discipline, as explained in *The Essence of Buddha*. For example, to advance from the level of arhat in the upper realm of the sixth dimension to the level of bodhisattva in the seventh dimension, you need to be reborn quite a number of times and live each life successfully. This is the reality.

Also, there is a harsh reality that more than 50 percent of the people living today end up in hell after they die. This means that having Buddha-nature within does not automatically lead to returning to heaven or attaining buddhahood. In terms of reality, this accords with the truth. Based on this fact, Tokuitsu criticized Saicho: "Your understanding of Buddha-nature is wrong. There are two kinds of Buddha-nature: theoretical Buddha-nature and practical Buddha-nature."

Tokuitsu presented his argument in the following way: "Theoretical Buddha-nature is the concept or theory that everyone has Buddha-nature. Indeed, it is true that as children of Buddha, everyone has Buddha-nature within them. I admit that. I have no intention of denying it because it is written in the Nirvana Sutra and the Lotus Sutra. But there is something called practical Buddha-nature. Although we have the Buddha-nature as a seed within us, unless we take good care of it by going through spiritual discipline, we cannot achieve buddhahood."

Of course, these two types of Buddha-nature were not part of Shakyamuni Buddha's original teachings, but what Tokuitsu said was theoretically correct. In theory, it is true that Buddha-nature or true thusness as essence exists within all people, but only when people put spiritual discipline into practice will their Buddha-nature shine forth and will they attain buddhahood. So it could be said that theoretical Buddha-nature is Buddha-nature as a theory of the Truth, whereas practical Buddha-nature is Buddha-nature that is actually realized through practice.

To conclude, we can interpret Tokuitsu's philosophy as, in Happy Science terminology, a *condition* in the law of cause and effect. For every effect, there is always a cause, but there also have to be certain conditions to produce the effect. In this case, spiritual discipline corresponds to the condition.

Just because you originally have Buddha-nature does not mean you will become a tathagata by leaving it as it is. If you could become a tathagata without polishing your Buddha-nature, Shakyamuni Buddha would not have undergone ceaseless self-discipline in pursuit of enlightenment. We need to refine our Buddha-nature through spiritual discipline before we can attain buddhahood.

Tokuitsu referred to the cause, condition, and result as theoretical and practical Buddha-nature. Even in light of Happy Science's teachings now, what Tokuitsu said was right. He was making the right criticisms.

6

The Philosophy of Five
Mutually Distinctive Natures

Sadly, Saicho could not accept Tokuitsu's theory at all. In other words, he understood the theory of Buddha-nature as existence as Buddha-nature having an immediate effect. He saw them as the same thing. If we analyze Saicho and Tokuitsu's debate, we can see how Saicho was consistent with the theory of one vehicle and the theory that everyone has Buddha-nature within. On the other hand, the Hosso sect (one of the Consciousness-Only schools), to which Tokuitsu belonged, advocated a philosophy of division according to the Five Mutually Distinctive Natures. Tokuitsu insisted on the validity of that philosophy while admitting the existence of theoretical Buddha-nature in all people.

The first of the five distinctive natures is the level of bodhisattva nature. Those who belong to this level have the nature of bodhisattva and come from the seventh dimension. (Some say bodhisattva refers to those who practice the discipline of the Six Paramitas.)

Below this is the level of hearer nature. These people are expected to become disciples of Buddha in the sixth dimension. (Some say that the main discipline of those who belong to this level is to meditate deeply on the Four Noble Truths of suffering, its cause, its extinction, and the Path.) Because hearers naturally seek to attain the state of arhat, most are considered to have come from the sixth dimension, but there are also some who belong to the level of bodhisattva yet practice the discipline of hearers; they are sometimes categorized as great hearers.

The third level is called solitary realizer nature. People who have the nature of solitary realizers like to discipline themselves in solitude rather than studying the teachings in an orthodox manner like hearers. (Some say that those who belong to this level mainly study the 12-fold chain of causality.)

To summarize these three levels, people have different soul tendencies: bodhisattvas devote themselves to saving others or engage in social reform like the Japanese monk Gyoki (668–749); hearers discipline themselves in an orthodox way through listening to the instruction of a teacher at a big temple, together with other monks or nuns; and solitary realizers prefer to live alone, seeking enlightenment in the mountains, like the Japanese monk Ryokan (1758–1831).

The fourth level is indeterminate nature. People at this level are similar to swing voters in an election; where they will return after death cannot be determined until they finish their lives on earth.

The fifth level is what could be called no-nature. This term sounds a little harsh; they correspond to the icchantika (a person who does not seem to have Buddha-nature). It means that there are some who hardly seem to understand the teachings of Buddhism or any other religion or have any belief in the other world. These people belong to no-nature, meaning they do not have Buddha-nature in the practical sense. There is a problem with this theory, but you can understand it as something similar to icchantika mentioned before.

The Five Mutually Distinctive Natures is the philosophy of the Hosso sect. This philosophy is correct to some degree. Although people endeavor to seek enlightenment, they all come from different levels and realms of heaven. So naturally, there will be a range in the level of enlightenment a person can achieve. If you want to return to a realm higher than the one you came from, you have to make enough effort to achieve it. It is also a fact that there are people with a low level of spiritual awareness. Some people had just got out of the hell realm, spending only a short while in heaven before they were born. In such cases, there is a high possibility that those people will lead dissipated lives and fall to hell again if they are left to themselves. The debate between Saicho and Tokuitsu included the question of whether we should acknowledge these sorts of differences between people.

7

Dogen's Doubts

In contrast, the one vehicle philosophy, with the Lotus Sutra as its main scripture, is considerably close to the idea of tathagata-garbha (an embryo of tathagata) in China—the idea that you are simply covered by a husk and once you remove it, a tathagata will instantly appear (Shinto also thinks in a similar way).

If you believe that "Everyone is just wrapped in a thin piece of cloth. Once they remove that, a tathagata will appear," then you will think it is ridiculous to make such a distinction between people; you will think that debating and investigating about such things, or the thought to discriminate people, is wrong. This is a debate that could take place even today. These kinds of thoughts were up against each other.

Over time, this dispute leaned in favor of the Tendai school and they eventually won. I believe this was largely because of the highly capable disciples that appeared later on.

Many new Buddhist schools were established in the Kamakura period, and many of these founders studied Buddhism at the Tendai head temple. The prominent

Japanese monks Honen, Shinran, Nichiren, Dogen, and Eisai had all studied there, so all of them fundamentally believed in the one vehicle philosophy. But after going through spiritual discipline at the temple, they began to have doubts and left the mountain to found their own sects. Because they couldn't agree with the teachings, they began their own movement.

In those days, Japan was beset by wars and famine, and people often starved to death and killed each other, so it was natural that the monks doubted the idea, "everyone had the seed of tathagata within and would naturally return to heaven." They thought, "In these circumstances, most people will go to hell. Isn't it the mission of Buddhism to save these people somehow?"

In this way, doubts were naturally raised, which then led to each of them organizing their own ideas and starting new Buddhist sects.

Dogen (1200–1253), the most well-known out of those monks, also had doubts. After learning the philosophy of innate enlightenment at the head temple, he felt that it made no sense.

The monks of the head temple preached innate enlightenment; they said, "Human beings are already enlightened before birth. So, there is nothing strange about them attaining buddhahood."

Dogen asked, "Shakyamuni Buddha attained great enlightenment after years of spiritual discipline. How do you explain this? Since ages ago, monks have been practicing spiritual discipline in all kinds of places; how do you explain the purpose of self-discipline? If we are originally enlightened beings and everyone can attain buddhahood, what is the point of spiritual discipline? If it is predetermined that everyone will achieve buddhahood, why do we discipline ourselves?" But no one at the head temple could give an answer to Dogen's question.

Dogen was advised by a senior monk to study abroad, so he went to China (Song dynasty) for several years. After studying there, he concluded that enlightenment could only be attained through spiritual discipline; so he founded Soto Zen Buddhism in Japan and underwent spiritual discipline.

The Pure Land School also started in the same way. Although the monks of this school took the one vehicle philosophy as the foundation of their doctrine, they thought people could still fall to hell, so they tried to find ways to prevent this. Similarly to how Dogen and others practiced the Zen meditation for self-discipline, the monks from the Pure Land School thought, "Simply put, people can be saved through faith. If people lacked the 'condition' factor in the laws of cause and effect, they wouldn't be able to attain buddhahood." The condition referred to, for example, reciting the sutra or having faith in Amitabha Buddha; through this condition, you can be saved by Buddha. Otherwise, you cannot be saved. This meant they considered faith to be the condition for the attainment of buddhahood.

Especially Honen (1133–1212)—known as the founder of the Japanese Pure Land School—endeavored to reinterpret the pure monism of the Tendai school as relative dualism. He honestly faced the darkness of human beings.

On the other hand, Nichiren (1222–1282), founder of the eponymous school, had a slightly different philosophy. While he criticized Honen's teachings that said, "You will be saved by reciting Namo Amitabha Buddha," as heresy, he put forward a new doctrine similar to his opponent's, stating that people could be saved through reciting, "Namu-myoho-renge-kyo."

In this way, Kamakura Buddhism was a group of new sects derived by the disciples who had the opportunity to study at Tendai head temple, and yet they questioned its teachings. This movement included religious reformation, of course, but it was also tainted with the mistaken philosophy that originated from Saicho. By then, very few believed in the Three Vehicles and everyone believed in the One Vehicle, so it is true that this toxic idea was included within.

8

The Problem of Equality and Fairness

Now, I would like to further explain Buddha-nature and buddhahood. This is eventually the same point about equality and fairness mentioned in *The Laws of the Sun*. It is the main point.

If we pursue the idea of the equality of all human beings, we reach the conclusion that all people equally have Buddha-nature or tathagata-garbha within. This is in fact a convincing and persuasive point of argument.

But some may wonder, if everyone has such equal potential, then does that mean everyone will be the same? If so, there would be no need for spiritual discipline on earth. In that case, what would be the meaning of the process of reincarnation we undergo through the past, the present, and the future? What about the causes and effects through our past, present, and future lives?

To answer these questions, we need to consider the matter from the perspectives of both equality and fairness. We all have equal potential, but because of the chain of cause, condition, and effect, we are treated fairly according to the effort we make and what we achieve.

If all people, regardless of whether they have killed or saved others, were to equally return to heaven, then heaven would become hell. If bodhisattvas lived together with those who kill people all the time, then that is no longer heaven but hell. That is why people return to different worlds. In this way, Buddhist philosophy degenerated over time due to a lack of correct understanding of equality and fairness. We must learn from this.

It needs to be made very clear that although everyone has Buddha-nature within, this does not mean they can all attain buddhahood. This is the conclusion.

As more than half the people are falling to hell in this present age, it is the mission of religion to save them. If we said everyone could achieve buddhahood because they all have Buddha-nature, it would mean we relinquished our mission as religion. It is a way of thinking that is too easy and wrong.

Many new Japanese religions that went astray use this logic. There are other Buddhist sutras on the philosophy of tathagata-garbha such as the Tathagatagarbha Sutra, which are considered a form of positive thinking. Presumably, Masaharu Taniguchi—founder of Seicho-no-Ie—also studied these kinds of scriptures.

In verse 70 of the Kasyapa Chapter of the Ratnakuta Sutra, there is an episode in which Shakyamuni Buddha says to a disciple, "Kasyapa, listen to me. When a candle is lit, the darkness disappears, but darkness does not come from one place and go to another. It does not appear or disappear from any direction, from north, south, east, or west. Moreover, the candle does not think, 'I will drive away the darkness.' Rather, when the candle is lit, the darkness naturally disappears in the light." Through this episode, you can clearly understand that modern positive thinking has its origin in Mahayana Buddhism. The idea of tathagata-garbha logically leads to positive thinking.

But tathagata-nature is not something that appears after simply peeling off chaff, for example; the reality is much different. One small misunderstanding can turn this idea into a simplistic philosophy of "having Buddha-nature means attaining buddhahood."

In short, although it is alright to interpret the philosophy of tathagata-garbha as encouragement, it would be wrong to say you can instantly become a tathagata by offering ritual prayers or holding a Buddhist scripture in your hands. If, however, you study the teachings of Buddha and try to put them into practice, then it might be possible for you to become a tathagata. But it would be wrong to say that you can become a tathagata simply by holding a sutra, reciting its title, or just changing your attitude. In reality, this is wrong; it is a weak spot in its logic.

In a religious group that branched off from Seicho-no-Ie, they teach that everyone will be saved and that they are destined to return to heaven. They say misfortune is simply the manifestation of negativity disappearing into thin air, so you don't have to make any particular effort to deal with these sorts of situations; things will get better on their own. But the leader of any religion who ignores the need for individual effort in this way will inevitably go to hell.

It was probably for this same reason that Saicho went to hell after his death. Although it was alright for him to say that everyone has Buddha-nature, it was a fatal mistake for him to one-sidedly draw the conclusion that everyone attains buddhahood. It is a historical fact that after Saicho's death, the Tendai innate enlightenment philosophy affirmed the very existence of present life and brought deterioration and corruption. For this reason, toxic water has undeniably been flowing within the stream of Japanese Buddhism ever since, for well over 1,000 years.

This was when the idea of self-discipline began to vanish. Even now, there still runs a big part of the philosophy that lightly interprets the attainment of buddhahood in the newly established religions that only seek worldly rewards. This poisonous water has its origin in the "everyone can become a buddha" philosophy. Just like the founder of the new religion mentioned previously, I believe Saicho himself is being made to take responsibility for this wrong philosophy. Although Saicho did not complete the Tendai innate enlightenment philosophy, he was the one who laid the foundations through his superficial interpretations of scriptures such as *The Awakening of Faith in Mahayana*, the Lotus Sutra, and the Flower Garland Sutra.

In short, it is wrong to think that just because you have Buddha-nature, you can easily become a tathagata without making any effort. A possibility is nothing more than a possibility, and the results you gain according to how you make use of your chances are not equal.

If we were to give everyone equal results, what would happen? In terms of politics, communism is an example. Eventually, people will stop working. In communist countries, everyone is supposed to be treated equally, regardless of how much effort they make. As a result, individual efforts are not justly rewarded, and there is no free competition. If the results are always the same no matter how much effort people make, they will lose their motivation and focus only on getting their share of welfare benefits. That would make an entire country go downhill.

Religion has experienced this phenomenon throughout its history, and I'm sure a similar phenomenon will follow in the world of politics too.

The ideas behind democracy are very close to the philosophies of "Buddha-nature exists in all people," "everyone can attain buddhahood" and the concept of tathagata-garbha. The ultimate political ideal is to be found in these philosophies, but if you reach for the ultimate ideal and it turns into an extreme theory, what could come next are corruption and a decline toward mobocracy. In short, seeking equal results will eventually yield such outcomes.

So, if we said that everyone could instantly attain the state of tathagata, religions would lose their mission and there would be no need for self-discipline. The Japanese Tendai school needs to be humble and repent for their mistakes. They led Japanese Buddhism into decline by going against the teachings of the T'ien-t'ai founder, Chih-i, and drove the innate enlightenment philosophy to the extreme. They ought to look back to the original teachings of T'ien-t'ai Chih-i, who adhered to the idea of acquired enlightenment through self-discipline.

9

Buddha-Nature as the Principles of Courage, Love, and Hope

If you try to pursue only a single aspect of the Truth in an extremely logical way, the outcome you arrive at could turn out to be the exact opposite of what you are aiming for. It is a wonder but societies, the lives of people, and Buddha's ideal have to do with how you balance such things, just like the two vectors of progress and harmony.

The idea that all people have Buddha-nature and tathagata-garbha can be used as the principle of courage. For example, to someone who is filled with despair, you can say, "Don't be so pessimistic. You, too, can be enlightened. You all can attain enlightenment." This will encourage the person to make an effort to develop spiritually.

Also, if you see a person who is spiritually advanced but arrogant and says, "You don't have Buddha-nature. Only I have Buddha-nature. Only I can become a tathagata or a bodhisattva," you can tell them, "You are wrong. You should be more humble and develop a loving heart toward others. Other people also have Buddha-nature." Here, the idea of Buddha-nature is used as the principle of love.

Moreover, thanks to the idea of Buddha-nature, there can be the high ideal of creating utopia on earth. It is because we believe that everyone is a child of Buddha and has Buddha-nature within that we could possibly create Buddha Land on earth. This is why we can make efforts for that goal. So the idea of Buddha-nature should also be used as the principle of hope.

The idea that essentially everyone has Buddha-nature is a religious principle, a religious truth that shows how things *should be*; so if it were to be understood as how things *actually are*, it would create major problems. Please be aware that this is a matter that could give rise to difficult problems.

This is the theme of this chapter, "Buddha-nature and Buddhahood." Things are not so simple. Simplistic ideas that pursue logical consistency alone will not necessarily turn out well but instead yield unexpected results. It is of course not good to have a dark philosophy that sees everyone as coming from hell, but it is also a crucial problem to simply assert that everyone is actually a tathagata as they are. It may cheer people up, but you must be cautious in turning it into a practical theory, for this could mislead people. I would like you to learn from history so that you will not make the same mistakes again.

Afterword for Part Two

Buddhism traveled from India to China and then to Japan. During the past two thousand and several hundred years, numerous Buddhist disciples endeavored to compile and convey Shakyamuni Buddha's teachings, precepts, and the commentaries known as the *tripitaka*. Those written compilations handed down to this day as Buddhist scriptures, therefore, include not only the teachings from the "golden mouth" of Shakyamuni Buddha himself but also the works of disciples done during those two thousand and several hundred years. Some of the records are correct, whereas others are mistaken. Some arguments were properly developed, whereas others were corrupted.

It is extremely sad for me, myself, to write and point out the mistakes in many of the Buddhist philosophies that have been passed down to this day. Nonetheless, I must do so. To revive Buddhism, which has become fossilized today, and imbue it with the breath of life, I cannot avoid this path.

The crucial themes that weren't mentioned in this book, *The Challenge of Enlightenment*, are scheduled to be taught later in another publication. Until then, I shall persevere together with you, the readers. That is my promise.

Ryuho Okawa
Master & CEO of Happy Science Group
June 1993

NOTES

1 *The Laws of the Sun* (New York: IRH Press, 2018)

2 The original order of Shakyamuni Buddha's Eightfold Path is Right View, Right Thought, Right Speech, Right Action, Right Living, Right Effort, Right Will, and Right Meditation. However, in this chapter, the order is arranged from a practical point of view.

3 The alaya-consciousness, which is translated by Hsuan-chuang (600–664), is a term used by the Consciousness-Only school and refers to what could be called the subconscious mind. The consciousness of a human being is seen by this school as consisting of eight consciousnesses—namely, the six consciousnesses of eye, ear, nose, tongue, body, and mind, the seventh one, manas-consciousness, and the eighth one, alaya-consciousness. The eighth consciousness, alaya, is considered to be the one that reincarnates. But in this classification, according to the relationship between the structure of the mind and the multi-dimensional structure of the other world (see Chapter Two of *The Laws of the Sun*), manas-consciousness corresponds to the astral body of the fourth dimension, and alaya-consciousness corresponds to the part that connects to the fifth dimension and above. This makes it difficult to explain Buddha-nature, or divine nature. The term alaya-consciousness is also called delusory consciousness. In *The Awakening of Faith* in Mahayana, Paramartha (499–569) translated the Sanskrit term alaya-vijnana as ariya-consciousness, which is considered to be a combination of true and delusory consciousnesses, including a level of consciousness as high as the eighth dimension and above. In the Lankavatara Sutra, which Zen Buddhism emphasizes, alaya-vijnana is translated as the storehouse consciousness and is considered to be the synonym for tathagata-garbha (see Chapter Six of Part Two). Note that in the She-lun sect of Paramartha, to resolve the confusion, a ninth consciousness is considered outside of alaya-vijnana called amala-consciousness. Amala-consciousness refers to the innate pure mind or the diamond aspect within the mind.

4 The Nagara River runs through Gifu Prefecture in central Japan, where the author gave this lecture in May 1992.

5 This lecture is compiled in *The Ten Principles from El Cantare VOLUME I* (New York: IRH Press, 2021).

6 The *sarvastivada* school ("existence school") is one of the most influential schools of Hinayana Buddhism. On the assumption that this world is composed of 70 elements or dharmas, and in an effort to explain the impermanence of all things in this world, it taught that these dharmas retain their identity in all three lives (through the past, present, and future lives). The followers were called sarvastivada, which literally means "those who insist on the existence of all things." Although they admitted the existence of the "dharma self," ironically, they denied the existence of the "human self" (identifiable human character). One of the reasons Mahayana Buddhism put forward the idea of emptiness was its intention to raise objections to the sarvastivada school, which recognized the existence of worldly dharmas. Note that *dharmas* in this context mean elements such as eyes, ears, taste, touch, perception, belief, ignorance, greed, pride, and acquisition.

7 The "seven Buddhas of the past" refers to Shakyamuni Buddha and his six past lives, who were all Buddhas. In chronological order, they are Vipasyin, Sikhin, Visvabhu, Krakucchanda, Kanakamuni and Kasyapa. These are the Indian names Shakyamuni Buddha used at the time to refer to his own past lives, such as Ra Mu, Thoth, Croud, and Hermes. But now, the seven Buddhas of the past are simply interpreted to signify faith in multiple Buddhas. To be precise, the story says that various Buddhas existed before Shakyamuni and that in the days of past Buddhas, Shakyamuni underwent spiritual discipline as a bodhisattva.

8 One of the Buddhist monasteries, Vikramasila, was burned down in AD 1203 by invading Muslims.

Part One

- Chapter One -
What Is the Spirit of Buddhism?

Japanese title: *Bukkyouteki Seishin to wa Nanika*
The Commemoration of the First Turning of the Wheel of Dharma,
Special Seminar on November 23, 1992
At *Tomakomai Shiminkaikan* in Hokkaido (Broadcasted Nationally)

- Chapter Two -
Freeing Yourself from Ignorance

Japanese title: *Mumyou kara no Dakkyaku*
from the Monthly *Koufuku no Kagaku* March 1992

- Chapter Three -
The Four Noble Truths

Japanese title: *Ku, Juu, Metsu, Dou*
from the Monthly *Koufuku no Kagaku* April 1992

- Chapter Four -

What Is Egolessness?

Japanese title: *Muga to wa Nanika*
from the Monthly *Koufuku no Kagaku* May 1992

- Chapter Five -

Emptiness and Causality

Japanese title: *Kuu to Engi*
from the Monthly *Koufuku no Kagaku* June 1992

- Chapter Six -

Karma and Reincarnation

Japanese title: *Gou to Rinne*
from the Monthly *Koufuku no Kagaku* July 1992

Part Two

- Chapter One -
Progress through the Middle Way

Japanese title: *Chuudou kara no Hatten*
Chubu region Special Lecture on May 17, 1992
At *Gifu Memorial Center* in Gifu Prefecture (Broadcasted Nationally)

- Chapter Two -
Hinayana and Mahayana

Japanese title: *Shoujou to Daijou*
from the Monthly *Koufuku no Kagaku* August 1992

- Chapter Three -
What Is Nirvana?

Japanese title: *Nehan to wa Nanika*
from the Monthly *Koufuku no Kagaku* September 1992

- Chapter Four -

Emptiness and Salvation

Japanese title: *Kuu to Kyusai*
from the Monthly *Koufuku no Kagaku* October 1992

- Chapter Five -

Egolessness from
the Perspective of the Middle Way

Japanese title: *Mugachuudou*
from the Monthly *Koufuku no Kagaku* November 1992

- Chapter Six -

Buddha-Nature and Buddhahood

Japanese title: *Busshou to Joubutsu*
from the Monthly *Koufuku no Kagaku* December 1992

For a deeper understanding of The Challenge of Enlightenment,
see other books below by Ryuho Okawa:

The Laws of the Sun [New York, IRH Press, 2018]

The True Eightfold Path [New York, IRH Press, 2021]

Invincible Thinking [New York, IRH Press, 2017]

The Philosophy of Progress [Tokyo, HS Press, 2015]

The Essence of Buddha [New York, IRH Press, 2016]

The Golden Laws [Tokyo, HS Press, 2015]

The Ten Principles from El Cantare Volume I [New York, IRH Press, 2021]

ABOUT THE AUTHOR

Founder and CEO of Happy Science Group.

Ryuho Okawa was born on July 7th 1956, in Tokushima, Japan. After graduating from the University of Tokyo with a law degree, he joined a Tokyo-based trading house. While working at its New York headquarters, he studied international finance at the Graduate Center of the City University of New York. In 1981, he attained Great Enlightenment and became aware that he is El Cantare with a mission to bring salvation to all humankind.

In 1986, he established Happy Science. It now has members in 166 countries across the world, with more than 700 branches and temples as well as 10,000 missionary houses around the world.

He has given over 3,450 lectures (of which more than 150 are in English) and published over 3,100 books (of which more than 600 are Spiritual Interview Series), and many are translated into 41 languages. Along with *The Laws of the Sun* and *The Laws Of Messiah*, many of the books have become best sellers or million sellers. To date, Happy Science has produced 25 movies. The original story and original concept were given by the Executive Producer Ryuho Okawa. He has also composed music and written lyrics of over 450 pieces.

Moreover, he is the Founder of Happy Science University and Happy Science Academy (Junior and Senior High School), Founder and President of the Happiness Realization Party, Founder and Honorary Headmaster of Happy Science Institute of Government and Management, Founder of IRH Press Co., Ltd., and the Chairperson of NEW STAR PRODUCTION Co., Ltd. and ARI Production Co., Ltd.

WHAT IS EL CANTARE?

El Cantare means "the Light of the Earth," and is the Supreme God of the Earth who has been guiding humankind since the beginning of Genesis. He is whom Jesus called Father and Muhammad called Allah, and is *Ame-no-Mioya-Gami*, Japanese Father God. Different parts of El Cantare's core consciousness have descended to Earth in the past, once as Alpha and another as Elohim. His branch spirits, such as Shakyamuni Buddha and Hermes, have descended to Earth many times and helped to flourish many civilizations. To unite various religions and to integrate various fields of study in order to build a new civilization on Earth, a part of the core consciousness has descended to Earth as Master Ryuho Okawa.

Alpha is a part of the core consciousness of El Cantare who descended to Earth around 330 million years ago. Alpha preached Earth's Truths to harmonize and unify Earth-born humans and space people who came from other planets.

Elohim is a part of the core consciousness of El Cantare who descended to Earth around 150 million years ago. He gave wisdom, mainly on the differences of light and darkness, good and evil.

Ame-no-Mioya-Gami (Japanese Father God) is the Creator God and the Father God who appears in the ancient literature, *Hotsuma Tsutae*. It is believed that He descended on the foothills of Mt. Fuji about 30,000 years ago and built the Fuji dynasty, which is the root of the Japanese civilization. With justice as the central pillar, Ame-no-Mioya-Gami's teachings spread to ancient civilizations of other countries in the world.

Shakyamuni Buddha was born as a prince into the Shakya Clan in India around 2,600 years ago. When he was 29 years old, he renounced the world and sought enlightenment. He later attained Great Enlightenment and founded Buddhism.

Hermes is one of the 12 Olympian gods in Greek mythology, but the spiritual Truth is that he taught the teachings of love and progress around 4,300 years ago that became the origin of the current Western civilization. He is a hero that truly existed.

Ophealis was born in Greece around 6,500 years ago and was the leader who took an expedition to as far as Egypt. He is the God of miracles, prosperity, and arts, and is known as Osiris in the Egyptian mythology.

Rient Arl Croud was born as a king of the ancient Incan Empire around 7,000 years ago and taught about the mysteries of the mind. In the heavenly world, he is responsible for the interactions that take place between various planets.

Thoth was an almighty leader who built the golden age of the Atlantic civilization around 12,000 years ago. In the Egyptian mythology, he is known as god Thoth.

Ra Mu was a leader who built the golden age of the civilization of Mu around 17,000 years ago. As a religious leader and a politician, he ruled by uniting religion and politics.

"The True Words Spoken By Buddha"

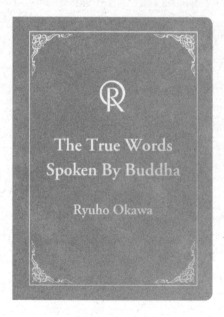

This is one of the greatest gospels for humankind; this sutra, which is the English version of Happy Science's basic sutra, was written directly in English by Master Ryuho Okawa.

Recitation CD

"The True Words Spoken By Buddha"

In this CD, Master Ryuho Okawa recites "The True Words Spoken By Buddha." Highly recommended to receive it together with the sutra book.

Lecture Book

The Lecture on "The True Words Spoken By Buddha"

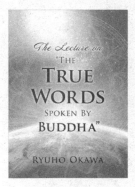

In this lecture, Master Ryuho Okawa recites the sutra and describes its meaning paragraph by paragraph, sentence by sentence. From the creation of this great universe, the spirit world, and reincarnation, to the reason of human existence, and the difference between love and mercy, you will be able to learn the profound messages and the meaning of "The True Words Spoken By Buddha."

→ Available to members only. You may receive them at Happy Science local branches and shoja (temples) worldwide. See p.378.

NEWLY RELEASED BUDDHIST TITLE

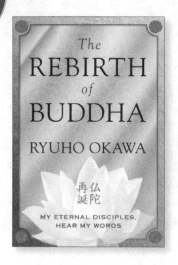

The Rebirth of Buddha

My Eternal Disciples, Hear My Words

Paperback • 280 pages • $17.95
ISBN: 978-1-942125-95-2 (Jul.15, 2022)

These are the messages of Buddha who has returned to this modern age as promised to His eternal beloved disciples. They are in simple words and poetic style, yet contain profound messages. Once you start reading these passages, your soul will be replenished as the plant absorbs the water, and you will remember why you chose this era to be born into with Buddha. Listen to the voices of your Eternal Master and awaken to your calling.

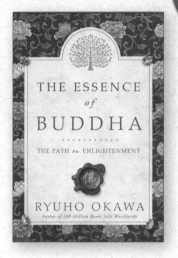

The Essence of Buddha

The Path to Enlightenment

Paperback • 208 pages • $14.95
ISBN: 978-1-942125-06-8 (Oct.1, 2016)

The essence of Shakyamuni Buddha's original teachings of the mind are explained in simple language: how to attain inner happiness, the wisdom to conquer ego, and the path to enlightenment for people in the contemporary era. It is a way of life that anyone can practice to achieve lifelong self-growth.

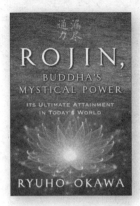

Rojin, Buddha's Mystical Power

Its Ultimate Attainment in Today's World

Paperback • 232 pages • $16.95
ISBN: 978-1-942125-82-2 (Sep. 24, 2021)

Rojin is one of Buddha's six divine supernatural powers: the ultimate ability to manage them all. Discover the secret of Ryuho Okawa who integrates these six mystical powers with common sense living. Learn how to develop and use *Rojin* to refine your soul and successfully manage your life.

The True Eightfold Path

Guideposts for Self-Innovation

Paperback • 272 pages • $16.95
ISBN: 978-1-942125-80-8 (Mar. 30, 2021)

Buddha's Eightfold Path is called 'the Secret Treasure of Mankind' as it has the tremendous power to transform one's life inside out to become a happier, compassionate and more productive person. Apply Okawa's 'True Eightfold Path' in today's world to make quality choices in life.

The Challenge of the Mind

An Essential Guide to Buddha's Teachings:
Zen, Karma and Enlightenment

Paperback • 208 pages • $16.95
ISBN: 978-1-942125-45-7 (Nov. 15, 2018)

A guide to exploring the infinite potential of our mind from Buddha's perspective. Okawa thoroughly explains the essential tenets of Buddhism. These teachings can elevate our state of mind to the core part of our Buddha-nature or Divine-nature and improve our capacity for love and enlightenment.

The Laws of Great Enlightenment

Always Walk with Buddha

Paperback • 232 pages • $17.95
ISBN: 978-1-942125-62-4 (Nov. 7, 2019)

Enlightenment is neither a sudden nor spontaneous state of being. Okawa explains that enlightenment must be worked on and maintained throughout one's lifetime. Okawa also criticizes the "sudden enlightenment" of Zen Buddhism and explains how work ability and enlightenment are interrelated.

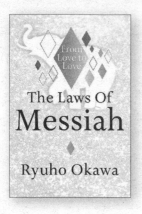

The Laws Of Messiah

From Love to Love

Paperback • 248 pages • $16.95
ISBN: 978-1-942125-90-7 (Jan. 31, 2022)

"What is Messiah?" This book carries an important message of love and guidance to people living now from the Modern-Day Messiah or the Modern-Day Savior. It also reveals the secret of Shambhala, the spiritual center of Earth, as well as the truth that this spiritual center is currently in danger of perishing and what we can do to protect this sacred place. Love your Lord God. Know that those who don't know love don't know God. Discover the true love of God and the ideal practice of faith. This book teaches the most important element we must not lose sight of as we go through our soul training on this planet Earth.

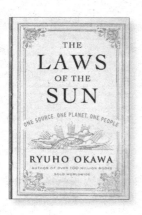

The Laws of the Sun

One Source, One Planet, One People

Paperback • 288 pages • $15.95
ISBN: 978-1-942125-43-3 (Oct. 15, 2018)

Imagine if you could ask God why he created this world and what spiritual laws he used to shape us—and everything around us. In *The Laws of the Sun*, Ryuho Okawa outlines these laws of the universe and provides a road map for living one's life with greater purpose and meaning. This powerful book shows the way to realize true happiness—a happiness that continues from this world through the other.

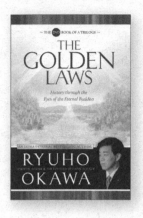

The Golden Laws

History through the Eyes of
the Eternal Buddha

E-book • 201 pages • $13.99
ISBN: 978-1-941779-82-8 (Jul. 1, 2011)

Throughout history, Great Guiding Spirits have been present on Earth in both the East and the West at crucial points in human history to further our spiritual development. *The Golden Laws* reveals how Divine Plan has been unfolding on Earth, and outlines 5,000 years of the secret history of humankind. Once we understand the true course of history, through past, present and into the future, we cannot help but become aware of the significance of our spiritual mission in the present age.

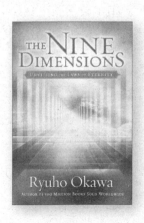

The Nine Dimensions

Unveiling the Laws of Eternity

Paperback • 168 pages • $15.95
ISBN: 978-0-982698-56-3 (Feb. 16, 2012)

This book is a window into the mind of our loving God, who designed this world and the vast, wondrous world of our afterlife as a school with many levels through which our souls learn and grow. When the religions and cultures of the world discover the truth of their common spiritual origin, they will be inspired to accept their differences, come together under faith in God, and build an era of harmony and peaceful progress on Earth.

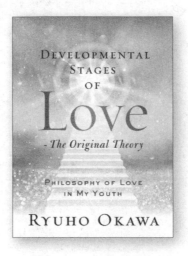

Developmental Stages of Love
- The Original Theory

Philosophy of Love in My Youth

Hardcover • 200 pages • $17.95
ISBN: 978-1-942125-94-5 (Jun. 15, 2022)

This book is about author Ryuho Okawa's original philosophy of love which serves as the foundation of love in the chapter three of *The Laws of the Sun*. It consists of series of short essays authored during his age of 25 through 28 while he was working as a young promising business elite at an international trading company after attaining the Great Enlightenment in 1981. This revolutionary philosophy, developmental stages of love, is the idea to unite love and enlightenment, West and East, and bridges Christianity and Buddhism. It is also the starting point of the global utopian movement, Happy Science.

OTHER RECOMMENDED TITLES

The Ten Principles from El Cantare Volume I
Ryuho Okawa's First Lectures on His Basic Teachings

The Ten Principles from El Cantare Volume II
Ryuho Okawa's First Lectures on His Wish to Save the World

The Power of Basics
Introduction to Modern Zen Life of
Calm, Spirituality and Success

The Laws of Happiness
Love, Wisdom, Self-Reflection and Progress

The Laws of Hope
The Light is Here

Invincible Thinking
An Essential Guide for a Lifetime of
Growth, Success, and Triumph

Twiceborn
My Early Thoughts that Revealed My True Mission

The New Resurrection
My Miraculous Story of Overcoming Illness and Death

For a complete list of books, visit okawabooks.com

MUSIC BY RYUHO OKAWA

El Cantare Ryuho Okawa Original Songs

A song celebrating Lord God

A song celebrating Lord God,
the God of the Earth,
who is beyond a prophet.

DVD
CD

The Water Revolution
English and Chinese version

For the truth and happiness of the 1.4 billion people in China who have no freedom. Love, justice, and sacred rage of God are on this melody that will give you courage to fight to bring peace.

DVD

CD

Search on YouTube

the water revolution for a short ad!

Listen now today!

 Download from
Spotify **iTunes** **Amazon**

DVD, CD available at amazon.com, and Happy Science locations worldwide

375

ABOUT HAPPY SCIENCE

Happy Science is a global movement that empowers individuals to find purpose and spiritual happiness and to share that happiness with their families, societies, and the world. With more than 12 million members around the world, Happy Science aims to increase awareness of spiritual truths and expand our capacity for love, compassion, and joy so that together we can create the kind of world we all wish to live in.

Activities at Happy Science are based on the Principles of Happiness (Love, Wisdom, Self-Reflection, and Progress). These principles embrace worldwide philosophies and beliefs, transcending boundaries of culture and religions.

Love teaches us to give ourselves freely without expecting anything in return; it encompasses giving, nurturing, and forgiving.

Wisdom leads us to the insights of spiritual truths, and opens us to the true meaning of life and the Will of God (the universe, the highest power, Buddha).

Self-Reflection brings a mindful, nonjudgmental lens to our thoughts and actions to help us find our truest selves—the essence of our souls—and deepen our connection to the highest power. It helps us attain a clean and peaceful mind and leads us to the right life path.

Progress emphasizes the positive, dynamic aspects of our spiritual growth—actions we can take to manifest and spread happiness around the world. It's a path that not only expands our soul growth, but also furthers the collective potential of the world we live in.

PROGRAMS AND EVENTS

The doors of Happy Science are open to all. We offer a variety of programs and events, including self-exploration and self-growth programs, spiritual seminars, meditation and contemplation sessions, study groups, and book events.

Our programs are designed to:
* Deepen your understanding of your purpose and meaning in life
* Improve your relationships and increase your capacity to love unconditionally
* Attain peace of mind, decrease anxiety and stress, and feel positive
* Gain deeper insights and a broader perspective on the world
* Learn how to overcome life's challenges
  ... and much more.

For more information, visit <u>happy-science.org</u>.

CONTACT INFORMATION

Happy Science is a worldwide organization with branches and temples around the globe. For a comprehensive list, visit the worldwide directory at *happy-science.org*. The following are some of the many Happy Science locations:

UNITED STATES AND CANADA

New York
79 Franklin St., New York, NY 10013, USA
Phone: 1-212-343-7972
Fax: 1-212-343-7973
Email: ny@happy-science.org
Website: happyscience-usa.org

New Jersey
66 Hudson St., #2R, Hoboken, NJ 07030, USA
Phone: 1-201-313-0127
Email: nj@happy-science.org
Website: happyscience-usa.org

Chicago
2300 Barrington Rd., Suite #400, Hoffman
Estates, IL 60169, USA
Phone: 1-630-937-3077
Email: chicago@happy-science.org
Website: happyscience-usa.org

Florida
5208 8th St., Zephyrhills, FL 33542, USA
Phone: 1-813-715-0000
Fax: 1-813-715-0010
Email: florida@happy-science.org
Website: happyscience-usa.org

Atlanta
1874 Piedmont Ave., NE Suite 360-C
Atlanta, GA 30324, USA
Phone: 1-404-892-7770
Email: atlanta@happy-science.org
Website: happyscience-usa.org

San Francisco
525 Clinton St. Redwood City, CA 94062, USA
Phone & Fax: 1-650-363-2777
Email: sf@happy-science.org
Website: happyscience-usa.org

Los Angeles
1590 E. Del Mar Blvd., Pasadena, CA 91106, USA
Phone: 1-626-395-7775
Fax: 1-626-395-7776
Email: la@happy-science.org
Website: happyscience-usa.org

Orange County
16541 Gothard St. Suite 104
Huntington Beach, CA 92647
Phone: 1-714-659-1501
Email: oc@happy-science.org
Website: happyscience-usa.org

San Diego
7841 Balboa Ave. Suite #202
San Diego, CA 92111, USA
Phone: 1-626-395-7775
Fax: 1-626-395-7776
E-mail: sandiego@happy-science.org
Website: happyscience-usa.org

Hawaii
Phone: 1-808-591-9772
Fax: 1-808-591-9776
Email: hi@happy-science.org
Website: happyscience-usa.org

Kauai
3343 Kanakolu Street, Suite 5
Lihue, HI 96766, USA
Phone: 1-808-822-7007
Fax: 1-808-822-6007
Email: kauai-hi@happy-science.org
Website: happyscience-usa.org

Toronto

845 The Queensway Etobicoke,
ON M8Z 1N6, Canada
Phone: 1-416-901-3747
Email: toronto@happy-science.org
Website: happy-science.ca

INTERNATIONAL

Tokyo

1-6-7 Togoshi, Shinagawa,
Tokyo, 142-0041, Japan
Phone: 81-3-6384-5770
Fax: 81-3-6384-5776
Email: tokyo@happy-science.org
Website: happy-science.org

London

3 Margaret St.London,
W1W 8RE United Kingdom
Phone: 44-20-7323-9255
Fax: 44-20-7323-9344
Email: eu@happy-science.org
Website: www.happyscience-uk.org

Sydney

516 Pacific Highway, Lane Cove North,
2066 NSW, Australia
Phone: 61-2-9411-2877
Fax: 61-2-9411-2822
Email: sydney@happy-science.org

Sao Paulo

Rua. Domingos de Morais 1154,
Vila Mariana, Sao Paulo SP
CEP 04010-100, Brazil
Phone: 55-11-5088-3800
Email: sp@happy-science.org
Website: happyscience.com.br

Jundiai

Rua Congo, 447, Jd. Bonfiglioli
Jundiai-CEP, 13207-340, Brazil
Phone: 55-11-4587-5952
Email: jundiai@happy-science.org

Vancouver

#201-2607 East 49th Avenue,
Vancouver, BC, V5S 1J9, Canada
Phone: 1-604-437-7735
Fax: 1-604-437-7764
Email: vancouver@happy-science.org
Website: happy-science.ca

Seoul

74, Sadang-ro 27-gil, Dongjak-gu,
Seoul, Korea
Phone: 82-2-3478-8777
Fax: 82-2-3478-9777
Email: korea@happy-science.org
Website: happyscience-korea.org

Taipei

No. 89, Lane 155, Dunhua N. Road,
Songshan District, Taipei City 105, Taiwan
Phone: 886-2-2719-9377
Fax: 886-2-2719-5570
Email: taiwan@happy-science.org
Website: happyscience-tw.org

Kuala Lumpur

No 22A, Block 2, Jalil Link Jalan Jalil Jaya
2, Bukit Jalil 57000,
Kuala Lumpur, Malaysia
Phone: 60-3-8998-7877
Fax: 60-3-8998-7977
Email: malaysia@happy-science.org
Website: happyscience.org.my

Kathmandu

Kathmandu Metropolitan City,
Ward No. 15, Ring Road, Kimdol,
Sitapaila Kathmandu, Nepal
Phone: 977-1-427-2931
Email: nepal@happy-science.org

Kampala

Plot 877 Rubaga Road, Kampala
P.O. Box 34130 Kampala, UGANDA
Phone: 256-79-4682-121
Email: uganda@happy-science.org

ABOUT IRH PRESS USA

IRH Press USA Inc. was founded in 2013 as an affiliated firm of IRH Press Co., Ltd. Based in New York, the press publishes books in various categories including spirituality, religion, and self-improvement and publishes books by Ryuho Okawa, the author of over 100 million books sold worldwide. For more information, visit okawabooks.com.

Follow us on:

f Facebook: Okawa Books   **⊙** Instagram: OkawaBooks

▶ Youtube: Okawa Books   **🐦** Twitter: Okawa Books

𝓟 Pinterest: Okawa Books   **g** Goodreads: Ryuho Okawa

———— **NEWSLETTER** ————

To receive book related news, promotions and events, please subscribe to our newsletter below.

🔗 eepurl.com/bsMeJj

———— **AUDIO / VISUAL MEDIA** ————

YOUTUBE   **PODCAST**

Introduction of Ryuho Okawa's titles; topics ranging from self-help, current affairs, spirituality, religion, and the universe.